Electronic Books and ePublishing

Springer-Verlag London Ltd.

Harold Henke

Electronic Books and ePublishing

A Practical Guide for Authors

Springer

Harold Henke, Human Factors and Usability Scientist
IBM Corporation, PO Box 1041, Niwot, CO 80544-1041, USA

British Library Cataloguing in Publication Data
Henke, Harold
  Electronic books and e-publishing : a practical guide for
  authors
  1. Electronic books 2. Electronic publishing
  I. Title
  002'.0285
ISBN 978-1-85233-435-2

Library of Congress Cataloging-in-Publication Data
Henke, Harold, 1956-
    Electronic books and epublishing : a practical guide for authors / Harold Henke.
    p. cm.
    Includes bibliographical references and index.
    Additional material to this book can be downloaded from http://extras.springer.com.
    ISBN 978-1-85233-435-2   ISBN 978-1-4471-0317-2 (eBook)
    DOI 10.1007/978-1-4471-0317-2

Z286.E43 H46 2001
070.5'797-dc21

                                                                    2001020858

ISBN 978-1-85233-435-2

http://www.springer.co.uk

© Springer-Verlag London 2001
Originally published by Springer-Verlag London Limited in 2001

Typesetting: Camera-ready by author

34/3830-543210 Printed on acid-free paper SPIN 10792007

Table of Contents

List of Illustrations

List of Tables

Preface

The following is a description of the paper book (pBook) and the electronic book (eBook) that is provided on CD ROM.

How this Book is Organized

Part One of this book is about the design of electronic books, the cornerstone of electronic publishing. It begins with a position statement that the paper book is not obsolete and that the format and organization of the paper book should be carried over to the electronic book until someone comes up with a better design. Following this statement, a description of literature on electronic books is presented to provide a foundation for the design of electronic books. From there, data gathered from usability testing is presented to support the design guidelines presented in this book. Finally, recommendations are provided for the design of an electronic book.

Part Two is about electronic publishing and begins by describing the importance of an odd sounding term metadata, which is data that is needed to describe the electronic book. Then a description of Digital Rights Management is presented which is technology that is needed to protect the content of the electronic book from unauthorized use. The next few chapters describe changes to the publishing business from the author and publisher's view as well as from the point of view of experts in the industry. After that, information is presented on the development of standards and on organizations that are active in providing information on the electronic book and publishing industry. Finally, some "how to" information is presented for authors who want to create their own electronic books using Microsoft Word and Adobe FrameMaker.

Differences Between eBook and pBook

This book is published primarily as a paper book (pBook) and as an electronic book (eBook) and as such some elements are only available in the eBook version, such as audio links. Here is a list of differences between the eBook and the pBook:

- The content is the same in both the eBook and pBook versions with the exception that the electronic version includes notes on the writing of this book. (Also, there may be some added content in the eBook due to printing schedules. Any extra content will be denoted in the eBook.) In essence, these notes are a behind-the-scenes look at how this book was written and are included only in the electronic book. These notes were not included in the pBook as they would clutter the book like footnotes and the reader would be forced to either read or ignore the notes. Simply put, with a pBook, you notice the footnotes, whereas in an eBook you can choose to read the note by taking a deliberate action, such as selecting the note to view or by simply turning the page and ignore the note.

- Cross-references and Uniform Resource Locations (URLs) have been converted into hyperlinks in the eBook version.

- Bookmarks (for the Adobe Acrobat Portable Data Format (PDF) eBook version) have been added only in the eBook version.

- Metadata (for the Adobe Acrobat PDF eBook version) has been added to support searching of the book and this data was added to the General Information section. This data is not included in the pBook version.

What is Included on the CD ROM

Here is a list of the content provided on the CD ROM; all eBook content is stored under the directory: eBooks.

- The complete book in Adobe Acrobat (PDF) format. Also

included are Acrobat Catalog indexes for use when using Acrobat Reader with Search.

- Selected chapters in Microsoft Reader (LIT) format.

- Selected chapters in Gemstar/NuvoMedia (REB) format.

- Selected chapters in MobiPocket format.

Usage Rules for the eBook

The Acrobat PDF file has the following usage rules applied to the eBook:

- Printing is prohibited because you bought the pBook and the eBook is included.

- Changing the document is not allowed. You can create annotations and set bookmarks but you cannot add or delete content to the eBook.

- Content copying and extraction is prohibited.

- The eBook is password protected and the password is provided in the readme.txt file.

Format of the CD ROM

The CD ROM is recorded in ISO 9600 format.

Revolution Before the Evolution

Evolution not revolution but personal revolution for me.

I started my publishing career in 1975 writing articles and pasting up the student newspaper and literary magazine at Scottsdale Community College, home of the Artichokes. I can still smell the mimeograph ink. After graduating from Arizona State University, I moved onto the journalism program at the University of Arizona, where they had installed electronic newspaper technology and the buzz around the newsrooms was what was going to happen to the people who set type. What would they do for a living?

In 1980, IBM offered me an internship to write technical documentation and try out this new publishing tool that required me to write my prose and surround it with these odd tags, like :p., :ul., which would magically cause the printer to format a paragraph and a bulleted (unordered) list. These tags were part of the General Markup Language (GML) based on the Standardized General Markup Language (SGML). My experience as an intern with GML led me to work on an assignment to help define the corporation format and structure for maintenance information manuals (service guides).

In 1984, I created my first electronic book using IBM's BookManager product, which at that time only operated on mainframes and "green screens" which were 3270 terminals. My "users" were system administrators and computer operators.

In 1990, I learned how to create electronic books using Interleaf and an IBM product called InfoCrafter. What was unique about this combination was not only did I create fully hypertext linked electronic books, I was able to integrate the book into the product so that the book became the product help system.

However, while these electronic books met with some popularity, the strategy was still to ship paper books with products and while electronic books were popular with some products, there was not a general acceptance throughout the corporation.

In 1994, I was working on documenting a product that was developed with a company in Sweden and they sent me their documentation as a "PDF" file. I had to ask what a PDF file was and they suggested I go to the Adobe website and download a copy of Acrobat Reader to read the electronic book. I was delighted because I could read the book online and conduct online searches, as well as print the book for intensive or deep reading. For this particular product, we wanted to ship a technical reference manual with the product but the product packaging was too small to fit a paper version in the box but we were able to ship an electronic version on a diskette. If we could not have shipped the electronic book, we would have had to ship the paper book separately or not at all. The electronic version provided real value to our customers.

In 1995, I conducted an experience to see if our customers would be interested in obtaining electronic books from our division's website. Since our books were in PostScript format, it was an easy step to convert our books into Adobe PDF files. Working with our division's Webmaster, we created a Digital Library, which we stocked with about 10 titles. We waited to see if our customers would find the library and download books in Adobe Acrobat format. The response was overwhelming and we began to add more and more titles as the number of downloaded books doubled monthly.

In 1996, I proposed that for one of our product lines, we ship only electronic books and no paper books. However, before we could do this, I was asked to prove, by usability testing, that users could perform any task with an electronic book that they could with a paper book. The results of that usability testing are included in this book; users completed every task and were satisfied with the electronic books. Based on the usability testing, and on the popularity of our Digital Library, the standard practice within in our division was to ship all books in electronic format.

In 1998, I was the leader of a task force that reviewed IBM's publishing strategy and we adopted the concept of shipping electronic books with all products. We created a product development team to provide tools such as better search and document management because our customers told us that they needed better tools to search through electronic books and manage collections of books.

Though none of this may sound revolutionary, I am reminded of the lead programmer, with whom I worked a few years ago on the development of a software application, who complained about our attempts to publish only electronic books. He said "I know what programmers want; they want a big stack of paper books, because that is how they know it's a real product". Through 20 years experience, I have seen a move from paper only books, to some acceptance of electronic books, to complete acceptance and demand for electronic books.

A Few Constants

Though technology has changed both the distribution and packaging of books over 20 years, a few constants have remained:

- For genres like technical documentation, users want electronic books for finding information quickly, and paper books for deep or intensive reading. They do not want one or the other, they want both.

- Whether the content is in electronic or paper book format, users want the content to be packaged using the book metaphor, which includes elements like a table of contents and index.

- Content is always what is important. Some technologies come and go and some technologies enable authors to add too many "bells and whistles" that detract from the content, but it is content that enables acceptance and use of electronic books.

Acknowledgements

Thanks to the following folk for helping out with this book: copyediting, Karen Borthwick, formatting assistance, Jim Ramsay, and technical illustrations, Patrick Rowe. Also thanks to Dr. Laurie Dringus for her efforts to hone my research skills. And thanks to the experts who contributed "content" to this book.

Part 1: eBooks

"There is an impression abroad that literary folk are fast readers. Wine tasters are not heavy drinkers. Literary people read slowly because they sample the complex dimensions and flavors of words and phrases. They strive for totality not linearity. They are well aware that the words on the page have to be decanted with the utmost skill. Those who imagine they read only for "content" are illusioned." Marshall McLuhan, 1967, from *Explorations*, Number 8, as reprinted in *Essential McLuhan*, 1995, edited by Eric McLuhan and Frank Zingrone

"Before ePublishing there has to be an eBook" Harold Henke, 2001

Part One is about the design of electronic books, the cornerstone of electronic publishing, and begins with a position statement that the paper book is not obsolete and that the format and organization of the paper book should be carried over to the electronic book until someone comes up with a better design. Following this statement, a description of literature on electronic books is presented to provide a foundation for the design of electronic books. From there, data gathered from usability testing is presented to support the design guidelines presented in this book. Finally, recommendations are given for the design of an electronic book.

Chapter 1: eVolution not Revolution

"The first printed works did not immediately change the appearance and form of medieval manuscripts; in fact, the early printers went to great lengths to produce precise imitations. So closely do some of the early printed works resemble manuscripts that they are virtually indistinguishable to the untrained eye." Ronald J. Deibert, *Parchment, Printing, and Hypermedia*, 1997

Papyrus, Parchment, Paper, and eBooks

Are papyrus, parchment, and paper the predecessors to electronic books or are electronic books simply a technology fad doomed to fail? Is the doomsday scenario as described by Henry Yuen, Chairman and Chief Executive of Gemstar-TV Guide International, where "hackers and inadequate reading devices" may cause a "crash landing before anything takes off electronically", a valid prediction (Italie, 2000a)?

Or are electronic books, in the words of Joseph Garber, in *Forbes* magazine, "gadgets, that have loser written on them" because the small display size causes users to have to scroll continuously, paragraph by paragraph, producing the effect of "trying to wade through an 800-page Tom Clancy opus printed on a mammoth roll of toilet paper..." (Garber, 2000).

On the other hand, is the electronic book an expected result of the impact the Internet has on the creation of an Information Age? And the beginning of the newest Gutenberg press?

Will the meeting (or collision) of paper and electronic books, in the words of Marshall McLuhan, result in "a moment of truth and revelation from which a new form is born" (McLuhan and Zingrone, 1995).

From Gutenberg to Gates

Since the advent of computers (especially personal computers), experts have predicted the paperless office, the rise of the electronic book, and the mass communication effect of the World Wide Web as the end of the paper book. Information forms like e-mail and webpages present us information in chunks that the experts predicted we would read on our computer displays or even have read to us by our audio assistants in lieu of being printed and read. However, the experts did not predict that technological advances would make it easy and inexpensive to print your e-mail or webpages, thus neither reducing the use of paper nor ending the paper book. Instead, the net result has been an increased usage of both.

One study stated, "world trends show that sales of paper increased with sales of computer networks." (Auramaki, *et al.* 1996). Another study by Liu and Stork (2000) stated that paper consumption for printing and writing increased 13% from 1970 to 1997, which corresponded to the pronouncement by Xerox researchers in 1970 that the dawn of the paperless office was imminent. However, thirty years later, Liu and Stork predicted "a long-term coexistence of paper and electronic documents" and, as the current generation of electronic books emerges, their prediction is more likely to be accurate than the prediction of Xerox researchers thirty years ago.

Is the Paper Book Dead?

Is the paper book dead and is the familiar format or package of information we call the book dead as well? With the advent of the Internet, some researchers have speculated that the package of information we call a book will be replaced by database publishing and collections of webpages. Furthermore, researchers speculated that both the book format and paper book will become obsolete given that information is readily available, 24 hours a day, 7 days a week.

Before the advent of the Internet, McLuhan in 1966,

postulated: "The tendency is for the book to cease to be a package and to become a custom-made information service tailored to the individual needs of the reader." (McLuhan and Zingrone, 1995.)

The predicted demise of the paper book has ignored that people, like you and I, were trained, since we were children, to read books, not chunks of information. Picking up a book and knowing how to read a book are for us a natural act, like riding a bicycle. As longtime users of books, we are highly experienced with books and our learning curve is very low; when we see a book, we know what to do with it. We read it. Therefore, at a minimum, the electronic book should be designed, initially, as an extension of the paper book to take advantage of our low learning curve and familiarity with the paper book.

Microsoft, in their description of Microsoft Reader, a software application used to view electronic books, pronounced the paper book as the perfect reading machine because the paper book had evolved and improved over centuries and for those reasons, Microsoft used the paper book as the blueprint to design Microsoft Reader. Among the features adapted from the paper book were: large margins; fully justified text, leading and kerning; and a book-like interface that utilized paper book metaphors.

Mitchell (1996) stated that if Gutenberg invented the printing press today, people would hail it as a major technological breakthrough. This is not an overstatement as the paper book has endured while electronic books have come and gone (more on this later in the book). If you imagine the paper book as a software application, the paper book would be a "killer application" because of these factors:

- Ease of use. Proven usability and very low learning curve. Most users have been trained to use the application since grade school.

- Platform independent. Operates on any operating system thus users can be assured that they can use the application, any time on any system.

- Open source code. Application developers (writers) can

develop books without using propriety source code.

- User interface. The user interface has been alpha and beta tested for hundreds of years.

- Drives sales of other applications and application plug-ins, such as audio and movies.

From pBook to eBook: Evolution not Revolution

If the paper book is a "killer application", then why replace it with another application that may not work as well nor provide more value? Muter (1996) observed that users are more efficient in reading from paper books than electronic books and that while improvements like higher resolution on display screens will help, "tinkering with modes of presentation will do little or no good past a certain point, a point which has been reached by the technology of the book. The book has evolved over several centuries to its present highly efficient form".

With that said, a revolution, perhaps appropriately called the Information Age and fueled by the Internet, is changing how books are published and how information is presented. Consider that Gutenberg's press enabled information to be packaged economically and in a format unseen, printed words instead of handwritten words. Handwritten books did not disappear immediately; instead, handwritten books moved from a mainstream industry to a cottage industry but both formats overlapped for over one hundred years.

The World Wide Web is influencing mass communications as significantly as Gutenberg's printing press influenced the availability of knowledge. The World Wide Web and information technology in general, such as inexpensive disk drives for storage, high resolution displays, large portable displays, inexpensive handheld computing devices, and so on, offer authors both a publishing platform and a means to distribute their works which have not been available before.

Key factors that are propelling the growth of electronic book technology include:

- Higher resolution displays. For example, the Rocket eBook utilized a 105 dots per inch display as compared to a standard 72 dots per inch workstation display resolution. Advances in display technology and, more importantly, in manufacturing techniques, are creating displays that match the resolution of paper and which are becoming less expensive.

- Longer lasting batteries. For example, users can read books on the Rocket eBook for up to 20 hours. Batteries also became smaller which supported form factors dedicated to reading electronic books.

- Software applications to create and view electronic books. Applications such as Adobe Acrobat Reader and Microsoft Reader can be used to view electronic books but they also provide tools that can be used with the most popular publishing applications to create electronic books. For example, both Adobe and Microsoft provide "plug-ins" for Microsoft Word that can create electronic books directly from Microsoft Word. Even high-end publishing design applications such as Adobe InDesign and QuarkXpress can be used to produce files that can be converted into electronic books.

- Multiple and low cost channels to distribute electronic books. In fact, there is an upsurge in self-publishing or vanity publishing as the low cost distribution of electronic or print-on-demand books enable an author to publish and distribute books inexpensively.

The information technology industry's push to develop and market electronic book readers, develop standards that define electronic books, and provide applications like Adobe Acrobat to turn any document into a viewable, electronic book, present you, as an author, with unlimited publishing possibilities. With publishing applications like Adobe FrameMaker and Microsoft Word, you can create sophisticated electronic books and distribute them to your readers via the World Wide Web or electronic book reader with an ease not seen before in the publishing industry.

However, with endless possibilities comes an endless opportunity to create hard-to-read electronic books as was experienced with the revolution of webpage publishing. Terms such as "lost in hyperspace" and "cognitive overload" connote the fact that often on the World Wide Web, design rules are lacking, not known, or simply not followed.

This guide was written with a central thesis: the book metaphor is a powerful metaphor that should not be discarded but should be used to enhance the design of electronic books until some other powerful metaphor emerges. The information presented in this book is a culmination of experience as an author and researcher and from information gathered through user surveys, user focus groups, usability testing, and participation by this author in industry groups and standards organizations.

Goals of this Book

This book is not a paean to the paper book. Instead this book provides authors with research on what features of the paper book should be incorporated into the electronic book as part of the evolution of the paper book (pBook) into the electronic book (eBook). The goals of this book are:

- Provide a brief history of the electronic book to help form a perspective on the development of the electronic book.

- Present research on the features that users of electronic books want in their electronic books and why these features are necessary.

- Describe the tools that are used to create electronic books.

- Discuss factors that influence the design of electronic books including Digital Rights Management, accessibility, and distribution.

Chapter 2: Once and Future History of eBooks

"So far, the focus of hypertext research has been on the development of new systems in a rather nontheoretical, technology-driven way. There have been few attempts to study the cognitive processes involved in reading hypertext or to provide a controlled evaluation of the impact of hypertext on learning." Jean-Francois Rouet and Jarmo J. Levonen, 1996, Studying and Learning with Hypertext: Empirical Studies and Their Implications, in Hypertext and Cognition.

Overview: Questions That Need Answers

This chapter provides an insight into factors that influence the design and use of electronic books and is organized to answer questions that define the factors that guide the design of electronic books.

1. What is the history of the electronic book? At the advent of the computer age, Vannevar Bush proposed an electronic book called Memex and another early innovator, Alan Kay, defined the Dynabook. Neither concept was turned into a product but in 1990, Sony's Bookman, was marketed but failed in the marketplace. Therefore, a history of electronic books is necessary to understand the foundation of current electronic books.

2. What is the definition of an electronic book? Electronic books can be defined as: a) hardware device, such as Softbook or Rocket eBook, that enables readers to view content; b) software applications, such as Acrobat Reader which are used to view content online; or c) the content that is viewed by a hardware device or software application. Each of these definitions affects the design of electronic books.

3. How are electronic books used? Electronic book design is influenced by the tasks users need to perform with their

electronic books such as the need to search for information to solve a problem versus the reading of a novel for leisure.

4. What is the relationship between paper books and electronic books? To understand whether paper book metaphors are useful in the design of electronic books, it is important to understand the relationship between paper and electronic books. What advantages do paper books offer over electronic books and what advantages do electronic books provide over paper books?

5. What is the conceptual foundation on the use of metaphor that describes the importance of metaphor to the design of electronic books?

6. What studies on electronic books have been conducted that relate to the use of paper book metaphors in electronic book design?

History of Electronic Books

The history of electronic books begins, in 1945, with the idea of a Memex, a device envisioned by Vannevar Bush, and continues to the present day with electronic book readers, such as the Rocket eBook and electronic book reader applications, such as Acrobat Reader and Microsoft Reader. Votsch (1999) stated that while the electronic book industry seems to be new, at least according to the coverage in newspapers and magazines, the industry is based on ideas that began with theorists, such as Bush and Kay and continued with ideas introduced with Project Gutenberg, a project dedicated to converting public domain books and documents into ASCII files, and to electronic book readers like the Sony Data Discman and Bookman. Votsch also cited Franklin Electronic Publishing who provided content for Bookman and for its own devices such as its online dictionary. Votsch stated that the next stage in the electronic book industry was publishing on CD ROM, such as Voyager Corporation, which provided multimedia titles. These early efforts led to the current crop of electronic book readers and electronic book applications.

Memex

Vannevar Bush, in 1945, described a hardware device called the Memex (the name Memex was chosen as the device supplemented human memory), which many researchers believe was the first description of an electronic book. Bush (1945) defined the Memex as a device that combined microfilm with a reader and screens for reading from a desk. The user could store their books, photographs, records, communications, and other paperwork that would be archived, indexed, and dynamically updated as needed. Bush envisioned the Memex as supporting book functions such as an index, annotations, and buttons to enable page turning. Though the Memex is considered a prototype of an electronic book, the Memex is more a concept for a document management system than a concept for an electronic book because of functions such as the cataloging of a variety of documents including magazines and newspapers .

Dynabook

The first prototype of a computer hardware device for reading books online was Alan Kay's Dynabook, which Kay proposed in 1968. It was based on the need for students to be able to access textbooks and course material using a portable computer that students could take with them wherever they needed the information. Kay's prototype was as much a forerunner of the laptop or notebook personal computer as it was a device to read electronic books. Johnstone (1999) described the progression of the Dynabook from idea to product by stating that the Dynabook first took form as a computer called Alto from the Xerox PARC laboratory. Kay referred to this as an interim step towards the Dynabook; the first commercially available version of the Dynabook was the GRID portable personal computer in 1984, which was followed in 1989 by Toshiba's Dynabook. Though Toshiba used the name Dynabook (only in Japan), the Toshiba Dynabook was one of the first personal computer laptops and was not designed specifically to read electronic books.

Superbook

An important prototype of electronic books that focused on design and included user-centered-design and testing was the Superbook, which was an electronic book, developed at the Bellcore Laboratory in 1985. The Superbook user interface consisted of four windows: 1) book title; 2) table of contents; 3) page; and 4) word look-up. Key features included a table of contents that was combined with a search engine so that when users searched for information, the results were tied into the table of contents to enable users to quickly locate the information (Egan, *et al.*, 1989).

Landauer (1996) described how researchers conducted usability testing on the electronic book including a test to determine if users could find information quicker using a printed book versus the Superbook. In usability testing of the first version of the electronic book, users found information quicker using the paper version. The researchers continued to re-design and test the electronic book and by the next version, users could find information quicker using the electronic version than the paper version. The researchers also tested users for knowledge retention and the electronic book users scored higher than paper book users. Landauer stated that the key finding of the Superbook project was that the design of electronic books should not mimic paper books but instead should incorporate functions of the computer, such as search, to provide a better medium for reading.

Sony Data Discman and Bookman

The first electronic book readers were marketed between 1990 and 1993 by Sony as the Sony Data Discman and Bookman but they were not successful (Feldman, 1995 and Keep & McLaughlin, 1995). The Sony Data Discman and Bookman were considered to be prototypes of the current personal digital assistant as they contained a CD ROM, memory, display, keypad, and because of their small size, were portable.

For the Discman, Sony marketed the device as an Electronic Book Player and created a proprietary system for publishing books that could be read on the Discman. Approximately 20 titles were available, with the Discman including the Library of the Future, Hutchinson's Encyclopedic Dictionary, and the Oxford Dictionary and Thesaurus. To create content that could be read on a Discman, authors needed to use Sony's Electronic Book Authoring System, which resulted in a proprietary file format. The Bookman, on the other hand, did not use Sony's proprietary system and could read any CD ROM formatted for the DOS operating system.

However both the Discman and Bookman were criticized for these limitations: the screen display was difficult to read except under the best lighting conditions and was small and could only display a portion of a page, the battery provided power for a limited time, search features were poor, the device could not be attached or communicate with other computers (though the Discman had the ability to display content via a television), and content was expensive and limited in availability. These limitations led to poor sales and within a few years, the Discman and Bookman were no longer sold and were withdrawn from the market.

Both products were the forerunner of current electronic book readers such as Gemstar/NuvoMedia Rocket eBook and Softbook. However, the founder of NuvoMedia, Martin Eberhard, referred to the Bookman as a "brick with a screen" (Lardner, 1999). Because of advances in technology, especially with batteries and displays, the current electronic book readers are very different than Sony's Bookman.

Gemstar/NuvoMedia Rocket eBook

The Gemstar/NuvoMedia Rocket eBook is an electronic book reader that has been commercially available since 1998. It was designed by NuvoMedia to provide a container to make information available to readers. The designers stated that the paperback was the most portable and popular book format so the Rocket eBook was designed to mimic the paperback in both form and function (McCusker, 1998). See Figure 1: Form Factors - Rocket eBook and Paper Book for an illustration that compares the Rocket eBook with a paperback. Paperback attributes provided in the Rocket eBook include the ability to turn a page, a menu button for table of contents, a progress indicator to depict how many pages are left to read, and the ability to underline text.

Figure 1: Form Factors - Rocket eBook and Paper Book

Everybook Journal

Everybook claims that the design of the Everybook Journal incorporated and supplemented important functions of the paper book by providing quick access, large library capability, and portability. The key paper book features supported are index, table of contents, highlighting, annotating, book marking, page numbering, and displaying two pages side-by-side.

The unique features offered by the Everybook Journal are the ability to copy a page or many pages from the electronic book reader to a printer or workstation for printing; the ability to read one page and create notes on a facing blank page. Two other unique features are that the Everybook Journal provides a form factor of 8.5 by 11 inches with two color displays so that when the electronic book reader is opened, the reader sees two facing pages, and it includes leather binding so that when it is closed, it looks like a leather-bound book.

IBM BookManager

First marketed in 1987 by IBM, BookManager was developed based on IBM's General Markup Language. This enabled BookManager files to be viewed on many different platforms as the book file could be formatted, automatically, to fit the display size. The BookManager format supported many paper book metaphors including a table of contents, index, headers, footers, page numbers, bookmarks, and annotations. The key feature of BookManager was that users could build libraries of books with bookshelves and thus extend the use of paper book metaphors from a single book to a library of books.

Acrobat Reader

Adobe Acrobat Reader was first marketed in 1994 and Adobe claims that users have downloaded over 100 million copies since then. The Acrobat Reader reads electronic books in Portable Data Format (PDF), based on Adobe's PostScript language; thus, one PDF file can be viewed online as well as printed. Because Acrobat was created from PostScript, a language designed to support printing, Acrobat Reader files maintained the original format of books designed for paper. Therefore, the online page was the same as the paper page and thus included typical paper book metaphors including annotations, highlighting, bookmarks, thumbnail views of pages, headers, footers, page numbers, leading, fonts, indexes, and a table of contents. Non-paper book features included search features and digital signatures. Acrobat also enabled users to view pages one page at a time, continuously and side-by-side, thus representing traditional book viewing.

In 1999, Adobe introduced Acrobat Reader with Web Buy, which was designed to facilitate purchasing electronic books in PDF format from distributor and provided copyright protection for authors and publishers. In 2000, Adobe purchased Glassbook and renamed the Glassbook Reader as the Acrobat eBook Reader.

Microsoft Reader

Microsoft began marketing Microsoft Reader, which it labeled as book reading software, in 1999 for personal digital assistants that used Microsoft's Pocket PC operating system and, in 2000, for any workstation that used Microsoft's Windows operating system. Microsoft proclaimed that the paper book, having evolved and improved for centuries, is the perfect reading machine and so Microsoft used the paper book as the blueprint to design Microsoft Reader. Among the features adapted from the paper book were: large margins; fully justified test, leading and kerning; and a book-like interface that utilized paper book metaphors.

The key features included: ClearType, which improved viewing on Liquid Crystal Displays (LCD) by enhancing the typeface to improve resolution; support for active reading, including ability to create bookmarks, create notes, and to highlight. Additionally, Microsoft Reader provided search functions, the ability to lookup a book from a collection of books, and tools to protect books from being read without purchase.

Comparison of eBook Readers with pBooks

Table 1: Comparison of eBooks and pBooks depicts that the leading electronic book readers and electronic book reader applications all support typical paper book features. Two of the products, Adobe Acrobat Reader and Everybook Journal, use the paper book metaphor extensively including side-by-side page viewing, while the NuvoMedia Rocket eBook uses a form factor modeled after the paperback book. Microsoft's Reader, while less exact as a paper book, also uses many of the paper book features.

While researchers have suggested that the use of paper book metaphors is only temporary until new metaphors are devised, it is apparent that the current electronic book reader and electronic book reader applications are designed to mimic the paper book.

Book Reader or Application	Use of Paper Book Metaphors
Acrobat Reader	Annotations, bookmarks, highlighting, page numbers, header, footers, index, table of contents, side-by-side page viewing.
Everybook Journal	Annotations, bookmarks, highlighting, page numbers, header, footers, index, table of contents, side-by-side page viewing.
IBM BookManager	Annotations, bookmarks, page numbers, header, footers, index, and table of contents. Libraries of books and bookshelves.
Microsoft Reader	Annotations, bookmarks, highlighting, page numbers, header, index, and table of contents.
NuvoMedia Rocket eBook	Annotations, bookmarks, underlining, page numbers, header, index, and table of contents. Form factor designed to match that of a standard paperback book.

Table 1: Comparison of eBooks and pBooks

Summary of the History of Electronic Books

The history of the electronic book is, to-date, filled with failures but the current products, which are both hardware and software products, offer more promise. One reason for potential success is that the companies who are marketing these products are well funded and have already gained acceptance in the market place, as is the case with Adobe Acrobat Reader.

Another key difference is that, previously, some of the concepts for electronic books never came to fruition, like the Dynabook, and other products failed due to technology, such as batteries that needed to be recharged frequently, but there are now more products offered in the last few years than in the previous 20 years.

Electronic Book Definitions

A review of the literature indicates that electronic books can be classified into two categories: a hardware and software device used to read content; and the content itself. Clister (1999) defined two types of electronic books: 1) the physical devices used to read books; and 2) the concept of viewing books online which includes the content and the tools used to view the content. Borchers (1999) defined an electronic book as "...portable hardware and software system that can display large quantities of readable textual information to the user and that lets the user navigate through this information." Lemken (1999) provided a simpler definition of electronic books as "...a mobile, physical device [used] to display electronic (digital) documents".

Borcher's and Lemken's definitions described a reading device that enables a user to view collections of documents or text where the content is represented by a book. Votsch (1999) stated that devices dedicated to reading books have been available since 1991 with the introduction of the Sony Bookman. Reading devices introduced in 1998 and 1999 include the Gemstar/NuvoMedia Rocket eBook and the Peanut Press Peanut Reader. While the Rocket eBook provides a single function, which is reading content, such as books and magazines, other devices, like the Peanut Press Reader, provide additional functions such as receiving and reading e-mail.

Common to these reading devices is content, in the form of books, to be read with the devices. Barker (1993) originally defined electronic books as a "...form of book whose pages were composed not of static printer's ink but from dynamic electronic information". Barker (1993) amended that definition to state that electronic books are a "...collection of reactive and dynamic pages of multimedia information". These collections of pages represent the content (books) that are read with a reading device.

Barker (1992) also provided another definition, which promoted the importance of metaphor use in electronic book design. Barker defined a metaphor as the ability of users to transfer familiar knowledge from one area, such as reading a paper book, to a less familiar area, such as reading an electronic book. Barker therefore defined an electronic book as "a generalized metaphor or myth that projects an image to both designers and users of being just like a [paper] book".

Clister (1999) stated that reading devices appeal to a limited number of computer users while the concept of reading a book online appeals to a far greater number of computer users. The concept of an electronic book, as defined by Clister, is more important than the machine used to read the book. Lemken (1999) acknowledged the need for well-designed books by stating that after 35 years of creating electronic text, paper is still preferred not because of the reading devices but because of "unsatisfactory interfaces and presentation principles" of the content itself.

Feldman (1995) wrote that the simplest definition of an electronic book is the hardware devices, such as personal digital assistants, laptops, mobile phones, and so forth, that are used to access the printed word, whether in the form of databases or structured electronic books. Feldman also wrote that a complex definition of electronic books is the adaptation of paper book metaphors and book-like features to create a new format for reading that re-interprets the paper book into a new, interactive, format.

Barker and Feldman provided a definition of electronic books as a generalized metaphor used to project an image of a paper book (book-like) to both designers and users. Within this research, their definition is the preferred definition of an electronic book. Regardless of how a user views the book, whether with a dedicated electronic book reader or with an electronic book reader application, users expect well-designed content (books) that they can use easily.

How eBooks are Used

The most common tasks that users perform with electronic books are to search for information, skim through the book for information, and perform active reading which includes annotating, and setting bookmarks. The following research describes how users read an electronic book.

Nielsen (1998a) described some limitations of electronic books and defined how electronic books are used by readers of technical manuals. Nielsen stated that reading from computer screens is 25 percent slower than reading from paper and that the design of electronic books is important to compensate for this limitation. Readers of technical manuals do not read manuals from cover to cover but search for specific information to solve a problem. Nevertheless, if the reader is learning how to use a product, or learning a new programming language, they will want to read large amounts of text in paper format. Nielsen stated that his research shows that users want the ability to print sections or entire books for extended periods of reading. Nielsen suggested that each electronic book should come in two forms: one for viewing and reading online and the other for printing.

Baldasare (1993) described the benefits of electronic books as easy to access, manage, store, and lower documentation costs. Users perceive electronic books as easy to search and more efficient than large libraries of information. The author stated that electronic books must match the ease of use of printed books which includes knowing where to locate navigation aids are such as table of contents and index and knowing how to use these navigation devices. The author defined four access features of electronic books: 1) table of contents; 2) electronic searches; 3) history functions; and 4) hypertext links, and listed features that should be incorporated into the design of electronic books as searching for information is a key feature in the use of electronic books.

Chignell and Valdez (1992) described research into the design of electronic books and focused on the finding of information, as this is a key feature of electronic books. They stated that there will be a gradual transition from paper books to electronic books and that it is important to use existing paper book functions such as a table of contents and index, because users know how to use these functions.

Price, Schilit, and Golovchinsky (1998) conceived a device to read electronic books that promoted active reading. They defined active reading as tasks such as underlining, highlighting, and commenting. Another design feature was the ability to make notes in the margin which could become the subject of a search query and which could be gathered into a collection of clippings that can be exported.

Fillion and Boyle (1991) stated that hypertext or electronic books have many advantages over paper because documentation, especially technical manuals, are well suited for non-linear presentation and so with good navigation and search functions, the hypertext book is superior to paper books. They reviewed a study of 16 hypertext documentation systems and noted nine usability issues: orientation; interface/presentation; search; navigation; index; links; literary paradigm, electronic augmentation; and customization/personalization. Of these nine issues, the following were ranked as most important: orientation (whether users became disorientated while looking for information); search; and index.

The Relationship between pBooks and eBooks

In many studies, paper and electronic books share similar features, for example, navigational devices such as a table of contents but also differences such as the resolution of paper versus a computer display. Within the literature, the key differences between paper and electronic books are often described thus: electronic books are used by people to find information and to perform active reading tasks such as annotating and bookmarking, while paper books are more often read for comprehension.

Nichols, Howes, and Jones (1995) investigated how students retrieved information from paper and electronic books and conducted a test where students searched for information in a large paper book (3,431 pages) and in a CD ROM with the same content. They stated that students retrieved information from paper by first using the table of contents and then the index. For electronic books, students preferred to use a search tool to find information but it was observed that students found it difficult to formulate effective queries with the search tool using the CD ROM version where students often resorted to using the table of contents and index provided on the paper version.

Guedon (1994) summarized two viewpoints which described the relationship between paper and electronic books: 1) electronic books are "radically" different from paper and any "reference to print" will make understanding the potential uses of electronic books very difficult; 2) electronic books are simply "print transferred to the electronic medium". Guedon believed that by classifying electronic publications, such as determining whether output from a newsgroup discussion represents an electronic journal versus a refereed electronic journal, the overall design of electronic books would be furthered.

In addition to classifying electronic books, a body of knowledge exists that defines differences in the use of paper and electronic books based on user tasks and genre. It has been suggested that paper is easier and more sensible to use when reading for comprehension while electronic books are better suited for finding information (Guedon, 1994 and Widenmuth, 1999). Further the type or genre of the content being read affects whether the content is better read as a paper book versus an electronic book. For example, a novel requires serial reading from the first page to the last page whereas a textbook may be read by chapter. Depending on the type of book being read, such as a novel, a paper book may be preferred over an electronic book (Borchers, 1999 and Widenmuth, 1999).

In a study related to a specific genre technical documentation, both printed and electronic, Smart, DeTienne, and Whiting (1998) surveyed users of a popular word processing program and found that when the users initially started using a new program, they preferred the printed book and if users encountered a serious problem with the program, the users preferred to use the printed books to get "unstuck". Smart et al. also observed that as the users became more experienced using the product, they used electronic books more often so the authors concluded that paper books are more useful to novice users and electronic books are more useful to experienced users.

Another factor is the task the user is trying to complete, as O'Hara and Sellen (1997) described in an experiment to determine how reading from paper differs from reading an electronic book where the task was for users to write a summary of what they had read. Two groups were formed with one group reading from paper, the other from an electronic book. The results showed that for writing about what was read, paper was more effective because paper provided better methods for annotation, quicker navigation, and could be laid out to suit the user.

Landauer (1995) identified nine research studies that showed users were able to find information quicker and more successfully using paper. One reason may be that paper books contain search tools that aid users in finding information. Landauer (1995) identified these paper book search tools as the table of contents, index, headings, and page numbers.

Mitchell (1996) wrote a book that was published electronically and in print and observed that paper has characteristics which make it easier to read and that if Guttenberg had not invented the printing press until now, people would hail the printing press and paper as a major technological breakthrough. Mitchell argued that the paper book included navigation tools in the form of chapters, index, and table of contents and that these navigation devices provided effective search capabilities. For the electronic book, a search engine was provided which replaced the need for an index and enabled Mitchell not to have to create an index. Mitchell believed the search engine provided more reliability for finding information because users could search for information without relying on the author's judgment of what terms belonged in the index. Mitchell noted the electronic book made following the paper book narrative format cumbersome and difficult and Mitchell recommended readers read the paper version first to understand the book and then read the online version for reference. Some unique features of the author's electronic book included: the ability of readers to enter comments and discuss comments with other readers and the author;

links to related material on the Internet; and book reviews.

Aikat and Aikat (1996) described their user-centered-design approach for online documentation with emphasis that readers of online documentation do not want to give up all of their print reading habits and that these habits are needed to provide ease of use for electronic books. They stated the following items must be shared between electronic and paper books: cross-references, chunking information, indexing, and a table of contents to ensure that users read an electronic book as easily as a paper book.

Chen and Willis (1997) defined textbooks as a manual written to provide instruction to students in either K-12 or college, and described how electronic books were better suited to textbooks than paper books.   Chen and Willis provided reasons why electronic books were better suited for textbooks than paper books: 1) incorporation of multimedia, 2) search, 3) group interaction between readers, 4) links to external resources; 5) interactive format versus the passive format of paper books; 6) enable students to build their own paths through the content, and 7) provide feedback to students while they read the electronic book. Chen and Willis believed electronic books were best suited for certain genres of books, such as textbooks, encyclopedias, and technical manuals, where there were large amounts of text and where readers did not expect to read the book from cover to cover but instead were expected to find specific information, quickly.

Graham (1999) described a reading system that was developed based on the premise that for over 200 years users have read books from beginning to end but today users instead skim documents for information. Graham summed up this change as vertical versus horizontal reading, with horizontal reading being more useful to cope with the vast sums of information available in electronic format. Graham stated that users still prefer paper because of resolution and flexibility but believed that with electronic books, which can be personalized for each user, these limitations would be mitigated. Graham stated that a key distinction between electronic books and paper books is the trend for readers to scan documents and not to read documents from beginning to end therefore an effective electronic book must provide users with information they want based on their input. Users want books built on demand to meet their needs and interests.

Muter and Maurutto (1991) presented a list of differences between reading online and on paper which included resolution and words per page. They stated that users read books in two ways: reading for comprehension and skimming for information. The authors believed skimming for information represented 30 percent of all reading. They conducted tests to determine if online books could support these activities. For the tests, Mutter and Maurutto used between 18 and 24 subjects (all college students) who performed tasks using electronic and paper books. The subjects were timed as they completed the tasks and then completed a series of questions to determine their comprehension level. Results showed that comprehension between electronic and paper books was the same but skimming was quicker using paper books. The authors questioned whether the results were accurate, as they believed skimming should be quicker using an electronic book rather than a paper book.

O'Hara and Sellen (1997) described an experiment on how reading from paper differs from reading online. The authors conducted this experiment because research on reading differences between paper and online had provided inconclusive and inconsistent data and research showed improvements in display technology which contradicted the notion that paper is far easier to read. The authors suggested that many of these studies were flawed because the studies did not focus on real user tasks but on variables such as display resolution. The experiment was created with the premise that user activities must be based on real tasks, which users perform when reading and which can be measured. The authors chose the task of text summarization as a common task that can be measured. Ten volunteers from their research and administration laboratory staff participated in the test with five subjects randomly assigned to reading from paper, and five to reading online. Subjects were asked to create a 200 to 300-word summary of the content, which was the same on both paper and online. The results showed that for writing about what was read, paper was more effective because paper provided better methods for annotation, quicker navigation, and could be laid out to suit the reader.

Schilit, Price, and Golovchinsky (1998) contended that current digital libraries only support a read-and-print model instead of a search-and-read model because there is no support for active reading. They described the XLibris project, which was designed, based on the book metaphor but expanding on what a traditional book can do by adding support for active reading including annotation. The following feature was adapted from the book metaphor: tangibility that enables a user to move through the book and determine how many pages are in the book. The reading device was page size and contained pressure strips to enable a user to riffle or skim through the book. Only one page at a time was displayed to help support the user's spatial memory (or sense of location in the book) and recognize familiar passages thus giving users a consistent sense of where they are in the book and reduce disorientation associated with electronic books and hypertext in general. Another aspect of the XLibris reading device is that it supports skimming by the user as key phrases highlighted are based on how often the phrase, or related phrases appears in the document. They concluded that by adding a variety of features to support active reading, these features could help reduce the time it takes to learn to read an electronic book.

Widenmuth (1999) reviewed studies on genres of books and how genre affects the tasks, the reader performs with a book. Widenmuth stated that defining tasks associated with electronic books is complex as an electronic book can support many tasks. For example, when reading a textbook, users may read serially but will also want to annotate and highlight sections. Widenmuth suggested two categories of activities: reading and support. For reading, specific tasks were: skimming, serial reading (quick), serial reading (study), reflective reading, proof reading, scanning/searching text (linear); scanning/searching text (non-linear); scanning/searching the table of contents or index; comparing with other books, and repeated reading. For support, specific tasks were: bookmarking, underlining/highlighting, annotation, note taking, outlining, copying, editing and revising text, linking passages, and applying the knowledge gained to complete an outside task.

Widenmuth suggested that, at a minimum, an electronic book must support tasks that include reading serially, scanning (skimming), annotating, and highlighting. Widenmuth also called for more research to define what types of tasks needed to be supported by electronic books otherwise electronic books would be viewed as less functional than paper books and thus ignored by users.

Conceptual Use of Metaphor in eBook Design

The use of metaphor to enable users to learn to use an application, product, or electronic book is based on the premise that metaphors can convey knowledge that a user already has in order to learn to use something new and unfamiliar. In electronic book design, the use of metaphor is often associated with using familiar paper book metaphors, such as a table of contents, to provide users with familiar devices to use in electronic books.

Kawasaki (1997) described how Apple software designers applied metaphors to design easy-to-use software. Kawasaki listed these rules on the use of metaphor: use metaphors from the real world, like a trash can or file folder, that can be easily understood and require little explanation; real world metaphors help users to feel comfortable as they have some understanding of the metaphor's use, as in the case of a trash can; good metaphors are universally recognizable and should be more recognizable than any text explanation could be, and do not use metaphors for the sake of metaphor, too much use can clutter the user interface and an ugly interface will kill a product.

Marcus (1998) defined metaphors as: "...fundamental concepts, terms, and images by which information is easily recognized, understood, and remembered. Metaphor includes essential means by which choices for command/control are communicated and the status of all data functions is depicted." Marcus stated that there are collections of metaphors associated with familiar objects and the following metaphor collections could be used in electronic book design: 1) document: books, chapters, bookmarks, figures; and 2) newspapers: sections, magazines, articles, newsletters, forms. Marcus stated that "good metaphors enabled users to comprehend, use, and remember information more quickly with greater ease and with deeper satisfaction by effectively managing the user's expectation, surprise, comprehension, and delight."

Perera, Hobbs, and Moore (1999) stated that users face two key problems when using hypermedia (and electronic books): cognitive overload and navigation overload. Cognitive overload is defined as users not being able to understand a system quickly enough which leads users to become confused as to the content and structure of information. Navigation overload is defined as when users interact with information via browsing or searching which results in users having to backtrack or retrace their steps to the last place in the electronic book, which causes users to lose track of the information they have read. They contended that metaphors provide a suitable means to prevent cognitive and navigation overload because metaphors transfer knowledge from a known domain to an unknown domain and can help users quickly develop an idea of how the application or product works.

Vaananen and Schmidt (1994) stated that much of electronic book design transfers the problems and responsibility of structuring the information in a meaningful manner from the author to the user and this forces the user to determine how to use the information. They suggested that these recommendations be incorporated into electronic book design: present more structure in the information space; apply user interface metaphors to make the visual presentation and user-environment interaction more easy to learn, intuitive, and understandable to the user.

Studies on the Use of pBook Metaphors in eBooks

Barker, Richards, and Benest (1994) investigated whether the use of paper book metaphors in electronic book design would improve user performance and satisfy user preferences. They created two electronic books: one that incorporated a paper book structure which consisted of page numbers, chapters, table of contents, and index, and another book that contained the same functions but without the use of metaphors, for example, the index was replaced with a keyword list and the table of contents was replaced with a section that described the contents of the book. They conducted a test consisting of two user tasks: reading, which consisted of reading for 20 minutes followed by a test to determine comprehension; and reference, which consisted of finding information. The test results showed that for reading, the use of paper book metaphors did not have an effect on user comprehension (scores were similar for both electronic and paper books) but the results did show that for finding information, the use of paper book metaphors improved user accuracy and enabled users to find information more quickly. Users did not show a preference for paper book metaphors when reading but did prefer paper book metaphors to assist them in finding information. The authors concluded that until an improved or more efficient or useful metaphor design emerged, authors should incorporate paper book metaphors into their design.

Catenazzi and Sommaruga (1994b) created the Hyperbook using paper book metaphors, as recommended by Barker, Richards, and Benest (1994), which incorporated metaphors such as book thickness, covers, table of contents, running heads, and page numbers. Hypertext links were provided for the table of contents, index, list of figures, and cross-references. Catenazzi and Sommaruga defined an evaluation test with four objectives: 1) determine ease of use; 2) find out if novice and experienced users could easily learn how to use the electronic book; 3) measure user satisfaction; and 4) determine future enhancements. To measure these four objectives, Catenazzi and Sommaruga used two groups of users, novice and experienced, and created three sets of tasks for each group: 1) a browsing task to find a general topic; 2) a searching task to find a specific piece of information; 3) an analysis task to read a topic and select the most relevant parts. Tasks were measured by quality (number of errors), time, and which tools were used and how often. Catenazzi and Sommaruga concluded that computer expertise did not affect user performance and that users easily learned how to use the electronic book because of the inclusion of paper book metaphors in the electronic book design. They noted that novice users relied more heavily on traditional navigation devices, such as the table of contents, than did experienced users. Catenazzi and Sommaruga also stated that their evaluation techniques could be used as a methodology to test the usability of electronic books.

Argentesi and Rana (1994) described two types of electronic books they designed: the Visualbook and Hyperbook. The Visualbook was created by converting a paper book into an electronic book, with the appearance closely matching that of a paper book to convey the cognitive background that the reader had already developed. The Visualbook included no hypertext links and was simply an image of a paper book that users could navigate by turning page by page. The Hyperbook was defined as a book that enabled readers to access text in a non-linear way. It was designed based on the paper book and included a book page format and book navigation tools, such as a table of contents, with search functions, and hypertext links. They created a prototype of a Hyperbook modeled after a paper book and which included paper book metaphors such as page numbers and indicators for the thickness of the book. After they completed a usability test, they added other paper book features such as annotations, bookmarks, and the ability to stack books upon each other once a book was opened, read, or set aside for future reading. They concluded that while there is merit at looking at other metaphors for electronic books, the paper book was proven to be the most efficient, effective, and flexible metaphor for organizing and presenting information and should be carried over to the design of electronic books. They also suggested that interactivity, such as hypertext links, was important, hence, the Visualbook was considered less usable than the Hyperbook.

Landoni and Gibb (1997) extended Catenazzi's and Sommaruga's Hyperbook model and created a prototype of an electronic book called Visualbook that was designed to capture the look and feel of text by incorporating fonts, footers, headers, justification, pagination, typefaces, and white space into the design. They created the prototype to validate the concept that the paper book metaphor provides an easy-to-use and powerful metaphor for electronic books. They conducted a heuristic review of their prototype using experienced and novice computer users and the review showed that both sets of users supported the use of paper book metaphors as helpful in finding information and thus validated the importance of using traditional print techniques, such as fonts, and typefaces, in electronic book design. Landoni and Gibb observed that novice users felt more strongly about the use of paper book metaphors than did experienced users. A reason for this is that experienced users have more expertise using the Internet and thus are more familiar with reading and accessing electronic books or similar types of electronic information on the Internet. Landoni and Gibb concluded that while experienced users may not be as dependent upon paper book metaphors as novice users, the use of paper book metaphors supports all users who are primarily interested in accessing information in an electronic book.

Crestani and Melucci (1998) described the process they followed to convert a large document into an electronic book. They stated that the reason for creating this study was that the usability of electronic books is difficult to determine even though many studies have been published. They believed an important design feature was to preserve the structure and features of the paper book because this would enable them to enhance the paper features of the book that they considered to be effective for users. They also maintained the page structure of the paper book along with the index. Crestani and Melucci confessed they did not test the model as they planned but claimed their design was based on a methodology which was tested in the design of other electronic books including: Guide, Hyperties, Emacs-Info, and Superbook.

Harmison (1997) described the creation of an electronic book to assist service personnel in repairing equipment. Harmison declared that the need for context or location to avoid disorientation in an electronic document is more important than in a paper document, hence the author included electronic footers to provide a contextual aid to users. Harmison also included table of contents and bookmarks, which could be applied not only to text but graphics as well. Harmison elucidated that a surprising observation from the testing was that users did not distinguish between the user interface of the application, in this case a text browser, and the actual content of the electronic book. Harmison wrote that users viewed the content and the viewer as the same application and thus if the content was difficult to use, then the viewer was considered difficult to use. Harmison concluded that effort must be placed on document (content) design as well as the user interface.

Instone, Teasley, Leventhal (1993) stated that while other

researchers have asserted that empirical studies are needed on the usability of hypertext books, of 82 studies presented at ACM conferences on hypertext, only 6 studies provided empirical results. They conducted research that compared an online encyclopedia with a paper version and then an improved online version. Their review of the literature suggested that the literature was spilt on whether paper was more effective than electronic books for reading. They tested a version of their encyclopedia with novice users and had them answer three sets of questions; the data was assessed in terms of accuracy and speed. From the test, the user interface for the electronic version was considered to hinder user performance as users did better in many categories using the paper version. Based on this test, the authors decided to re-design the user interface to see if user performance could be improved. For the second test, they tested 12 novice users and used the same questions (the content of the encyclopedia was not changed, only the user interface). The results of the second test showed that the user interface re-design, which focused on providing better navigation tools, improved both accuracy and speed over the original design and the paper version. They noted that only novice users were tested and that experienced users might have provided different results.

Koons, O'Dell, Frishberg, Laff, (1992), described the IBM *Computer Sciences Electronic Magazine* as a hypermedia version or translation of a paper magazine designed for readers of magazines like *Scientific American* and *Discovery*. The design was based on the premise that users were familiar with the magazine format so the hypermedia version should carry over paper magazine metaphors including cover, article, departments, and sidebar. They assumed users would bring experiences with video, print magazines, and computer games to bear when using the hypermedia magazine. They conducted usability testing to: 1) determine how users read and used the paper magazine; and 2) determine if users could use the interactive magazine as well as a paper magazine.

Data was logged on users' actions, comments, and requests for help, usability problems, task completion, and time taken to complete the task. For the first test of the paper magazine, users were tested with two conditions: unfamiliar and familiar. The same conditions were applied for the test of the interactive magazine. For the first test, all subjects completed all tasks and for the second test, 20 percent of those familiar, and 63 percent of those unfamiliar, with the material failed to complete one or more tasks. Those familiar with the material completed the tasks almost twice as quickly than those unfamiliar with the material. They provided a list of usability problems that included: lack of table of contents (number one usability problem), and busy-looking screens. The findings indicated that the design did not remain true to the paper magazine and/or VCR metaphor and for this reason; the user's learning curve was higher than expected. They re-designed the interface and added more paper magazine metaphors including: table of contents, index, and glossary, and more VCR metaphors such as, pause, play, and reverse. They concluded that the closer the user interface matched the real world object, such as a VCR, the more usable the magazine was to the users. An interesting observation was that several of the usability problems were the result of the content itself, including problems like headings that were not meaningful, too much text on a page, and confusing navigation.

Landauer (1996) described the Superbook project which included the design and test of an electronic book. Landauer and others converted a 550-page paper student textbook into an electronic book. They used two groups of students: one group used the paper version, the other used the electronic version to test which group could find information more quickly and which group would receive higher grades. The first design showed students could find information faster with the paper textbook than the electronic textbook because of poor navigation. Landauer updated the design to include highlighting of search results which improved usability. The results proved that students who used the electronic textbook received higher grades due in part because searching for specific text provided a context for helping users to improve retention by spending more time reading than searching for information. Landauer observed that the Superbook design suggested that electronic book design should not be based on making the screen look exactly like paper but should instead harness the power of the computer, such as search technology, to provide more efficient functions than paper.

Louka (1994) stated that the usability of hypermedia is an important problem but that there is little empirical research, even though the problem is well documented in the literature. Louka stated that hypermedia would not be widely accepted until the usability issues were overcome. Louka reviewed articles on many facets of hypermedia design including information structure and, most relevant to this book, use of metaphor. Louka described the research on the use of a book metaphor with hypermedia and provided citations from those researchers such as Nielsen who do not favor using the book metaphor to those who do. Louka stated that the majority of researchers supported the use of book metaphors in the design of hypermedia. Louka declared that books converted from existing books should use the familiar book metaphor if the new book does not take advantage of hypertext features. Louka observed that while many researchers, such as Benest, Catenazzi, and others believed the use of the book metaphor enabled users to become familiar quickly with new technology, other researchers, like Nielsen, believed users would quickly outgrow the book metaphor. Louka concluded a new set of metaphors was needed for the design of hypermedia.

Moll-Carrillio, et al. (1995) described a project to create Tabworks, which was a user interface designed to enhance the standard Windows 3.1 user interface, with a goal of providing a book metaphor to serve as a method to store and organize documents and applications. Prototypes were built which included elements such as covers, pages, tabs, bookmarks, paper clips, pockets, and sticky notes. The authors performed a walk-through test followed by the talk aloud method with users. User testing resulted in many changes to the user interface to improve task completion and the final design included a three-ring binder, tabs, and covers which mimicked a notebook or paper book for organizing information.

Nielsen (1998) stated that electronic books will never be a good idea, even if resolution on computer screens is a good as paper, because the "book is too strong a metaphor" which causes writers and designers to create electronic books for the wrong reasons. Nielsen opined: "electronic text should not mimic the old medium and its linear ways. Page turning remains a bad interface." Nielsen proposed that electronic books should use technology to create a new way to read information and focus on using functions like search and hypertext linking to provide a "more powerful user experience than a linear flow of text". Nielsen also believed that linear reading, which began with papyrus is no longer valid as readers do not have time to read from the first page to the last page but want to find information presented dynamically and "under the direct control of the reader, not the author."

Summary of the Relationship of eBooks to pBooks

The definition of what is an electronic book is important because users tend to believe that the content, application, or hardware device are all the same thing, an electronic book. But there are three definitions worth noting: 1) the content itself; 2) the software application, such as Adobe Acrobat Reader or Microsoft Reader which is used to read content; and 3) the hardware device that is used to read content.

It is important to separate the content from the application or hardware device used to read the content because the content itself may be poorly designed while the application or hardware device is well designed. For example, if the content does not include navigational aids, such as a table of contents and index, then it is important that the application or hardware device provides some tool to search the content to make up for the lack of these navigational aids. If not, then users will not enjoy their reading experience.

With regards to the use of electronic books, which is tied to the type or genre of content, the literature shows that genre is very important in determining how users will perform reading tasks, such as annotation. For the textbook and technical documentation genre, users want to use electronic books primarily to find information quickly but for "deep reading", or reading for comprehension, users prefer paper. Regardless of genre, users can learn to use an electronic book software application or electronic book hardware reader more quickly if the content incorporates familiar paper book metaphors such as chapter headings, table of contents, indexes, page numbers, thickness indicators, and so on. The reason for this is that the use of metaphor to convey familiar knowledge to a new situation, such as learning to use an electronic book hardware reader, reduces the user's learning curve.

Some researchers have argued that designing electronic book content using the paper book as a guide is too limiting to the development of electronic books and will cause developers and designers to ignore valuable features, like audio and multimedia. This will also curtail the development of new metaphors for electronic books. Most researchers disagree and argue that the paper book has been developed over hundreds of years and as such is the product of extensive usability testing. These researchers believe that the best way to ensure acceptance of electronic books by users is for the electronic book to evolve from the paper book by incorporating many of the familiar paper book metaphors in the design of the electronic book until new models or metaphors for electronic books emerge.

Chapter 3: Centering the User in the eBook Design

"Poor design makes us feel like idiots. We blame ourselves [but we] should blame it on the designers and encourage them to seek help. If half the money spent on focus groups went instead to usability testing, the world would be a much less frustrating place." Jim Louderback, 2001.

Electronic Books and UCD

This chapter provides usability data gathered from surveys and usability testing to describe how users use electronic books and what features are important to them. The data presented here represents the output of studying and designing electronic books by following the user-centered-design (UCD) process.

Preece *et al.* (1994) defined user-centered design as an "approach which views knowledge about users and their involvement in the design process as a central concern". A key characteristic is that any product, whether a television or eBook, must benefit from asking users what features they want in the product and how the product should function. However, authors, unless they are writing a peer-reviewed book, may not include users in their "design" process; the features that should be included in an eBook, such as a table of contents, represent the research from the UCD process.

The usability research presented in this chapter was derived directly from interviewing, surveying, and testing users, which are fundamental elements of the UCD process, to determine their preferences for features and functions in an eBook.

Real World Users and Their Tasks

Much of the research on the usability of eBooks has been conducted with students as participants and while students are certainly potential eBook users (especially in the textbook genre), they are not representative of "real world users". In this section, data is presented that was gathered from users who need to use an eBook to perform tasks and from service technicians who use an electronic service guide as part of their job.

1. A usability test was conducted to verify that users could use an electronic book in place of a paper book to perform everyday tasks. This test was designed so that users, who represented customers who perform tasks with a printer, such as fix a paper jam, could use an electronic book instead of a paper book. Since these users would not normally use the electronic book on a daily basis, it was important to verify that when they needed to perform a task, they could indeed find the information they needed to support the task.

2. A survey was conducted of 187 service technicians who use an electronic book on a daily basis to assist them to repair printers. These users rely on an electronic service guide to be able to do their job and, as such, the usability of the electronic service guide has an impact on their jobs.

Usability Test of an eBook

The purpose of this usability test was to determine if users could use an eBook instead of a paper book to complete common tasks performed with a laser printer. The printer was shipped with a CD ROM that contained a variety of information, including eBooks. The usability test was designed to make sure users could complete tasks, such as finding information on how to order a toner cartridge, using the electronic book instead of a paper book. This usability test provides insights into how users will want to use an electronic book and how their use dictates design principles.

Objectives

This test focused on the usability and retrievability of a *Printer User's Guide* in electronic book format. The electronic book format was defined as the *Printer User's Guide* formatted as an

Adobe Acrobat Reader Portable Data Format (PDF) file shipped on the CD ROM with the printer. The test focused on how easily customers could use Adobe Acrobat Reader to find and view information in the *Printer User's Guide* to complete specific tasks. The objectives of this test were twofold:

1. To ensure that participants could perform tasks using an electronic book instead of hard copy.

2. To determine how easily information could be retrieved from the electronic book and provide input to the technical writers to improve retreivability.

Evaluation Method

Representative users (participants) were given a number of typical tasks to perform. Additionally, retrievability tasks were completed to determine how easily participants could find information using the electronic book with Adobe Acrobat Reader. These participants needed the skills of a key operator to perform these tasks; they also needed to be familiar with CD ROMs. (Typical skills included: loading paper, setting printer settings, such as to reduce toner usage, and solving errors, such as print problems or paper jams.)

Each participant was asked to perform all tasks. Task-completion time, user mistakes, users' subjective impressions of the tasks, product difficulty, and users' comments were gathered and reported for each task.

Participants

For this test, four people with skills matching those of typical printer users were recruited from a local temporary employment agency. An additional participant, identified as Participant 5 (P5) was also used but Participant 5 had previously completed part of another test. Participant 5 was asked not to complete Operator Panel Tasks and Hardware Tasks, as these tasks were very similar to a previous test. In addition, a walk-through test was completed by another user with little printer and electronic book experience.

The results of the walk-through test are not included in this analysis but verified that the tasks and test were appropriate and valid.

Participant Summary

Here is a summary of the participants:

- All participants had attended college: three had graduated from college and one had completed two years of college.

- The participants had little experience installing computers or computer equipment at home or at work.

- All participants had experience using office copiers and desktop laser and inkjet/ribbon printers.

- All participants had experience using Apple or Windows 3.0/3.1 or Windows 95 operating systems.

- None of the participants had experience using Adobe Acrobat Reader.

- Most participants had some experience using the Internet and three out of four participants had downloaded a file from the Internet.

Test Scenario and Tasks

At the start of the test session, each participant was given a brief description of the purposes of the test and an overview of the tasks to be performed. Following this overview, each participant was given access to a computer, printer, the CD ROM, and the test printer. Participants completed each task as listed in the Tasks section. After completing the test, each participant was asked to complete a brief questionnaire describing the usability of the *Printer User's Guide* electronic book.

The following are the tasks that the participants completed.

Participants were asked to write down the page number(s) where they had found the information needed to complete each task. This enabled me to verify that the participant did indeed use the electronic book to complete the task.

Start Tasks

The Start Tasks were included for these reasons: 1) to determine how easily participants could find the *Printer User's Guide* on the CD ROM and 2) to encourage participants to become familiar with the Adobe Acrobat Reader user interface and to discover functions like the Find (search) function and Print function.

1. Insert the CD ROM into the CD ROM drive and then locate the *Printer User's Guide*.

2. Open the *Printer User's Guide* so you can view the manual on your computer display.

3. Search for information about the EPA Energy Star program in the *Printer User's Guide*.

4. Print the page where the EPA Energy Star logo appears.

Operator Panel Tasks

1. Use the operator panel menus to print a configuration page.

2. Use the operator panel to set the printer to save energy after one hour.

3. Use the operator panel menus to set the printer to continue automatically when certain errors occur.

4. Verify that these settings have been changed by printing a configuration page from the operator panel.

5. Use the operator panel menus to set the printer so that the print area extends from one edge of the paper to the other edge, with

no margins. (This value should be set for PCL print jobs.)

6. Use the operator panel menus to prevent printer from automatically switching to the auxiliary tray if another tray runs out of paper.

7. Use the operator panel menus to prevent blank pages from printing.

8. Verify that the settings have been changed by printing a configuration page from the operator panel.

9. Use the operator panel menus to print a list of PostScript fonts that are installed on the printer.

Hardware Tasks

1. Load letter size (green) paper into the auxiliary tray.

2. Using the operator panel menus, setup the printer to use paper from the auxiliary tray.

3. Print a configuration page to make sure the printer is using the green paper from the auxiliary tray.

Retrievability Tasks

1. You need to order a replacement toner cartridge. Find the toner cartridge part number.

2. The printer operator panel displays error message 45 Option Error. Locate information that tells you how to solve this problem.

3. You need to know if you can print Monarch size envelopes. Locate information that tells you what size envelopes you can print on the printer.

4. The printer is printing pages in all black. Locate information

that tells you how to fix this problem.

5. The printer is printing pages too light. Locate information that tells you how to set the printer to print darker.

6. You have been asked to determine how many pages have been printed on the printer. Locate information that tells you how to determine the number of pages printed on the printer.

7. You have heard this printer has a feature that can increase the number of pages you can print from a toner cartridge. Locate information that tells you how many pages you can print from a toner cartridge when using this feature.

8. You decide you want to use this feature to use less toner and you want to know how to set the printer to use this feature. Locate information that tells you how to setup the printer to use this feature.

Participant Satisfaction Summary

Below are the participant responses to the tasks they completed. The participants used the following scale: 1=Very Satisfied; 2=Satisfied; 3=Neutral; 4=Dissatisfied; and 5=Very Dissatisfied.

Participants are identified as Participant 1 (P1), Participant 2 (P2), Participant 3 (P3), Participant 4 (P4), and Participant 5 (P5). Note: Participant 5 was asked not to complete the Operator Panel Tasks and Hardware Tasks as Participant 5 had participated in a previous test.

Start Tasks

Questions	Participants					
	P1	P2	P3	P4	P5	Average
Finding the User's Guide on the CD ROM?	4	2	3	4	4	3.4
Using Adobe Acrobat Reader?	3	3	3	4	3	3.2
Locating the Energy Star heading and logo?	2	1	2	4	2	2.2
Printing the Energy Star heading and logo page(s)?	1	1	2	4	1	1.8
Comments						Participants
Hard time finding the User's Guide and I did not realize where to look at first at all.						P1
No comments.						P2
Small print difficult to read and more difficult to find specific headings.						P3
Trouble getting started and finding where to start.						P4
No comments.						P5

Table 2: Usability Test - Start Tasks Results

Operator Panel Tasks

Questions	Participants					
	P1	P2	P3	P4	P5	Average
Printing a configuration page?	4	2	2	3	N/A	2.75
Setting up the printer to continue automatically when an error occurs? (Autocontinue function)	4	2	2	3	N/A	2.75
Changing the paper source to auxiliary tray? (source=auxtray)	3	1	2	2	N/A	2.00
Setting up the printer to print edge to edge?	1	1	2	2	N/A	1.50
Setting up the printer not to print from the auxiliary tray when the other paper trays are empty?	3	2	2	2	N/A	2.25
Setting up the printer to prevent blank pages from printing?	4	3	2	2	N/A	2.75
Printing an error log?	2	2	5	2	N/A	2.75
Comments					**Participants**	
Easier as I went along. Once I remembered to use the Find command, it was very simple. Sometimes I skimmed along things to find an item and those times I would totally pass it up.					P1	
No comments.					P2, P3, P4, P5	

Table 3: Usability Test - Operator Panel Tasks Results

Hardware Tasks

Questions	Participants					
	P1	P2	P3	P4	P5	Average
Loading letter size paper in the auxiliary tray?	5	1	2	2	N/A	2.50
Setting up the printer to use paper from the auxiliary tray?	3	1	2	3	N/A	2.25
Comments	Participants					
I did not know what let-lef means and could not find it.	P1					
No comments.	P2, P3, P5					
Provide a diagram of where auxtray is located with directions.	P4					

Table 4: Usability Test - Hardware Tasks Results

Retrievability Tasks

Questions	Participants					
	P1	P2	P3	P4	P5	Average
Finding the toner cartridge number?	1	1	3	2	2	1.80
Solving the 045 option error message?	1	1	2	2	3	1.80
Determining if the printer supports Monarch size envelopes?	1	1	2	3	3	2.00
Determining what to do if the printer prints pages in all black?	5	1	2	3	3	2.80
Determining how many pages were printed on the printer?	3	1	2	3	4	2.60
Learning about how to save toner?	5	2	3	2	3	3.00
Configuring the printer to save toner?	3	3	2	2	2	2.40
Comments	Participants					
Hard to find because there was no keyword list.	P5					

Table 5: Usability Test - Retrievability Tasks Results

Task Completion Times

The following table lists how long it took each participant to complete a set of tasks. All values are expressed in minutes and the average time was rounded up to the next minute.

	P1	P2	P3	P4	P5	Average
Start Tasks	9	8	5	19	3	9
Operator Panel Tasks	46	42	24	54	N/A	42
Hardware Tasks	14	7	2	10	N/A	11
Retrievability Tasks	28	19	28	19	24	24
Total Time	97	76	59	102	N/A	86

Table 6: Usability Tasks - Completion Time

Participant Comments

Comments were provided by the participants on a form called Participant Comments. After the test was completed, the participants were asked questions related to the test; their comments are provided below:

Question 1: Please list any positive comments you have about the printer, CD ROM, or User's Guide.	Participants
When it was easy to find using the Find option in the tool, it was great and much easier to retrieve than a book. It was also much easier with the cross-references.	P1
It was very detailed. I liked how it had step-by-step instructions, never assuming that you already knew each step. The operator's panel on the printer was very easy to use.	P2
The CD ROM was very useful. It was thorough and useful. Everything I was asked to do was clearly labeled in the index and only once did I have to check more than one page to find what I needed.	P3

I like the option to click on the Index headings to find more information. Although this is a great option, it should be made more clearly at the beginning of the User's Guide. Information is grouped together nicely.	P4
Soft copy book was setup well. Generally easy to find info on a topic.	P5

Table 7: Usability Test - Participant Feedback – Question One

Question 2: Please list any negative comments you have about the printer, CD ROM, or User's Guide.	Participants
It is not as portable as a book, which is nice to have next to the printer. The index is not as easy to use as one in a book and the same with the table of contents.	P1
It was sometimes hard to find something specific. The Find button should search for all occurrences of what you are looking as when I searched for blank pages, it only gave me locations of blank pages because of printer problems, not how to skip them.	P2
The CD ROM had small print [that was] difficult to read. [Had] to zoom in and out all the time.	P3
The user should be given basic information to start. Diagrams should be provided more frequently. Clearer statements about whether controls are directly on the printer, keyboard, or User's Guide.	P4
Certain topics go by different names in soft copy than on paper. [Page count and machine information on configuration page]. Hard to go back to a page when I was in index such as back to letter p. [Found using the back and forth arrows in Adobe Acrobat Reader confusing.]	P5

Table 8: Usability Test - Participant Feedback – Question Two

Question 3: Do you have any suggestions on how to improve the printer, CD ROM, or User's Guide?	Participants
Some way to get direct access to each letter in the index by possibly having it up on the tool bar rather than going straight to the last page. I also did not know where to type in the page number or to go back to the previous page display (such as in the case you have the back button that you can use). For the printer as well, I saw that the arrow and forward and back but I could only get the menu to go forward.	P1
Improve the Find button.	P2
Is there anyway to jump to a specific page number other than clicking in the index. Also is there a way to return to normal page size directly after zooming in.	P3
Make the Find option more effective. Easier browse capability.	P4
No comments.	P5

Table 9: Usability Test - Participant Feedback – Question Three

Participant Interviews

The following are comments gleaned from participants when interviewed after the test:

Comments	Participants
Participant thought that the title of the book was not very useful and that the book should be started when the CD ROM is inserted into the CD ROM drive. Thought the index was not very useful and needed more entries, for instance, blank pages not in index. Felt that if had to look for a long time or read much, then the soft copy would be harder to use than a hard copy book. Wanted to find the name of the function that saves toner. Had to look for density to get a hint on how to set the printer to save toner.	P1
Participant found it hard to find the book tab and hard to locate the User's Guide. Did not think the Find function worked well, said it was hit and miss. Found the table of contents hard to use to get to specific items and felt the index was hidden at the back of the book.	P2

Participant found it hard to find the books tab as did not think of books as something on a CD ROM. Wanted an icon of a book on the CD ROM interface. Finding the toner cartridge number was hard. Also determining how to set the printer to save toner was hard and found a hint in the toner specifications. In addition, page numbers were a distraction because page numbers on the page do not match the page numbers Adobe Acrobat Reader uses. You cannot go from one page number to another using the page number on the page.	P3
Participant expected to find a tab for the User's Guide on the CD ROM user interface. Felt that using books, hard copy or soft copy was counter-productive. Said books looked scanned like an image and not like an application. Wanted index at front of book not at back of book. Felt pressured to find things fast. Also said not an instruction kind of person and does not like to read any instructions, prefers to do first, and then read something, if stuck.	P4
Participant found it difficult to find the User's Guide and thought the User's Guide should have its own tab on the CD ROM user interface. Felt there should be a book icon on the CD ROM user interface. Prefers hard copy, as Participant likes to flip through a book. Starts at table of contents and then goes to index. Did not use the Find function. Found finding how to determine the printer page count very difficult.	P5

Table 10: Usability Test - Participant Interviews

Recommendations from Usability Study

Suggestion	Reason
Increase the number of index entries.	The index serves as a word list similar to word lists used by search engines. Participants were able to move quickly through the index and jump directly to the task. The index helped the participants overcome the limited search functions of the Adobe Acrobat Reader Find function. Overall, a key usability fact is that the number of index entries should far exceed the traditional measurements used for pBooks. The index is vital for successful use of any eBook. When the participants discovered the index and found the term or concept they were looking for, the time it took to complete a task decreased significantly.
Consider adding a link to the index at the beginning of the book as a tip to soft copy users.	This could be added in the first chapter or as part of the preface. Users stated they wanted the index at the beginning of the eBook, not at the end. At a minimum, they wanted a very clearly identifiable link to the index at the beginning of the eBook.

Table 11: Usability Study Recommendations

User Preference for Finding Information in an eBook

I conducted research over a two-year period to determine how users preferred to find information in an electronic service guide. The studies were conducted by surveying service technicians who used eBooks as part of their jobs to service and repair printers. 187 service technicians over a two-year period participated in the survey. The service technicians were asked to rank which features they used most often to find information in the eBook. The features were:

- The table of contents which consisted of hypertext linked entries.

- The index which consisted of hypertext linked entries.

- The search utility which was Adobe Acrobat's Find feature.

- The bookmarks where were Adobe Acrobat bookmarks.

User Preference	Method
98% (1998); 94% (2000)	Table of Contents
88% (1998); 87% (2000)	Index
79% (1998); 79% (2000)	Search Utility
53% (1998); 34% (2000)	Bookmarks

Table 12: User Preference for Finding Information in an eBook

An important factor in both of the studies was the consistent preference of users for the use of a table of contents and indexes for finding information in the eBook. These two studies were conducted over a period of two years with similar audiences (service technicians) and the results showed that both sets of users preferred finding information using a table of contents and indexes.

What Users Want

In the usability test and surveys, user's preferred methods for finding information and navigating through electronic books were to use the table of contents and index. Following those methods, they used the old reliable method of "thumbing" through the pages. Therefore, for genres of electronic books, such as technical manuals and textbooks, chunking information into small units with many headings (as well as indexing) is important for usability. In addition to the transition from reading paper books to electronic books, the electronic books must include the old reliable table of contents and index.

Chapter 4: The Medium as Message: It's a Book

"The latest Rocket eBook instrument is very good, better than sitting at your computer, but it still pales next to the 500-year-old technology of the printed book". Nora Rawlinson, 2000, as reported by Hillel Italie, Associated Press.

What Should an eBook Look Like?

Figure 2: A Fanciful Future of eBooks

What the Experts Think

At the National Institute of Standards and Technology eBook Conference: Changing the Way We Read, I conducted a quite unscientific survey to determine which features the experts who attended the conference would want in their own eBook. 17 experts, most of whom had been contacted by e-mail before the conference, participated in the survey.

Definition of eBook Features

Here is the list of features with definitions that the users were asked to choose as either important or unimportant.

Feature	Description
Annotations	Make comments in the electronic book
Application link	Enable users to link to applications such as a spreadsheet
Audio	Support for music or voice clips to be played
Back cover	Back cover representing the end of the book
Book reviews	Enable users to write a book review for other users
Bookmarks	Enable users to create their own bookmarks
Bulletin board	Enable users to post comments about the book for other users to read and respond to each other
Chapter headings	Headings to indicate beginning of a chapter
Division headings	Headings indicate beginning of a division
E-mail	Provide access to e-mail form to contact author or other readers
External links	Provide links from other Internet locations to the book
External hypertext links	Links to sources available outside the electronic book that can be accessed via the Internet
Figure captions	Description of figures

File attachment	Ability to attach a file to the electronic book
Footers	Include text such as page number, title, or date updated that appears at bottom of each page
Form(s)	Provide forms such as an order form
Front cover	Cover representing the beginning of the book
Glossary	Definition list of terms
Headers	Include text such as page number, title, date updated, which appear at bottom of each page
Headings	Headings to indicate importance such as headings to supplement chapter and division headings
Highlight	Markup words or sections of a book
Index	Provide traditional index with hypertext links
ISBN identifier	Provide ISBN number
Page numbers	Indicate position within the book
Search	Ability to search within a book for a phrase or word
Spine	A spine with book title and other nomenclature
Stamp	Enable users to rubber stamp a book such as for review or confidential
Table captions	Provide a table captions with tables
Table of contents	Provide table of contents which would be hypertext linked
Tabs	Indicate the start of a new chapter or section in a book
Thickness indicator	Provide users with a sense of how thick the book is
Title page	Title page
Watermark	Graphic or text that appears across a page of text
3-D effect	Provide depth to text or graphics including rotation, angle, and texture
Video	Ability to play video clips

Table 13: Definition of eBook Features

Ranking of eBook Features

Here are the rankings of each feature and, as you can see, the preferred features match the user preferences as described in Chapter 3: Centering the User in the eBook Design.

Feature	Sum	Rank	Percent
Search	14	1	100.00%
Annotations	13	2	85.20%
Audio	13	2	85.20%
Bookmarks	13	2	85.20%
Chapter headings	13	2	85.20%
Highlight	13	2	85.20%
Division headings	12	7	76.40%
Glossary	12	7	76.40%
Index	12	7	76.40%
External inks	11	10	55.80%
Figure captions	11	10	55.80%
Footers	11	10	55.80%
Headers	11	10	55.80%
ISBN identifier	11	10	55.80%
Table of contents	11	10	55.80%
Title page	11	10	55.80%
Front cover	10	17	50.00%
Headings	10	17	50.00%
Application link	9	19	38.20%
Page numbers	9	19	38.20%
Table captions	9	19	38.20%
Video	9	19	38.20%
Internal link to external sources	8	23	29.40%
Lists	8	23	29.40%
Thickness indicator	8	23	29.40%
Attachment	5	26	23.50%
Back cover	5	26	23.50%
Book reviews	4	28	8.80%
Bulletin board	4	28	8.80%
Form	4	28	8.80%

Watermark	4	28	8.80%
3-D effect	4	28	8.80%
E-mail	3	33	2.90%
Stamp	3	33	2.90%
Spine	2	35	.00%

Table 14: Ranking of eBook Features by Experts

Additional Features Suggested by the Experts

Here is a list of features which were suggested by the experts:

Feature	Description
Boolean and/or natural search	Boolean are operators like AND; natural search is the ability to phrase a search string as a question.
Copyright page	This feature should have been included on the original list as it is still a requirement for any type of book.
Export annotations	This is a feature common in electronic book reader applications. It enables users to export their annotations from the eBook to another source, such as a word processor.
Graphical indexes	The concept of using illustrations and pictures to enable users to navigate the eBook by selecting a picture that represents information within the book.
Ranked search	The ability to rank search hits by relevance; common for most search tools.
Reflowable text	Reflowable text is text that can be resized, automatically; to fit the user's display. For example, a reflowable eBook could be resized, automatically, to be displayed properly on a personal digital assistant as well as on a 21-inch display. The key to reflowable text is that the content must be in a tagged-based language, such as XML, to preserve the structure of the content.

Search annotations	The facility to search annotations, which is a common feature in electronic book reader applications.
Time bombs (trial)	The capacity to preview an eBook for a period of time before the user loses access to the eBook. This feature enables the mass marketing of eBooks by simply making a trial version of the eBook available. A very common marketing tactic for electronic games and software.
Wireless access	The capability to download an eBook via wireless protocols onto a device, such as cell phone.

Table 15: List of Additional eBook Features

Perfecting the Book

Opinions from scholars and data gathered from users shows that:

- Scholars believe that in order to evolve from the pBook to the eBook, initial eBook design should mimic the pBook by incorporating as many pBook metaphors as possible. By mimicking the pBook, users will learn to use eBooks more quickly and will accept the transition quicker.

- Users have shown in both survey and usability studies a preference for paper book metaphors to navigate and find information in eBooks. The reason for this is that they are used to using the devices that have been developed and tested over hundreds of years of use.

Of course, perhaps the eBook and the pBook will coexist forever. Book buyers, according to a survey conducted by *Publishers Weekly*, showed that out of 1,140 consumers who had purchased a book online, only four consumers believed that eBooks would replace pBooks. Only 60% knew about eBooks in the first place (Italie, 2000).

For other thoughts on the perfection of the eBook, read Chapter 8: A View from the Gallery, Question Two: Evolution or Revolution? for the views of experts in the electronic book and publishing industry.

Design Odds and Ends

The following is a description of some design odds and ends that should be considered when designing an eBook.

Fonts and Typefaces: Back in Black

One of the earliest complaints about articles and books published on the World Wide Web was the proliferation of fonts and typefaces used within webpages. Users found they could easily mix any number of fonts and typefaces with text on a single page and they could add features such as animation and color to the text. Since many of the users were not trained in design and did not have publishing backgrounds, users with backgrounds in graphic design and publishing began to nominate the most flamboyant or poorly designed content for poorest design or least usable content.

Another factor that came out of the proliferation of articles and books on the World Wide Web was that some typefaces provided excellent resolution on paper but less excellent resolution on displays. This led to two developments: 1) typefaces created specifically for viewing on displays; and 2) technology to enhance viewing text on displays, specifically, Adobe's CoolType and Microsoft's ClearType.

For authors, the important aspect is that when writing a book, you have to be aware that some fonts will view better on a display and will look less impressive on paper. This means that you have to know how your book will be distributed whether electronically or paper or both. Depending on which distribution method will be used most often should dictate what types of fonts you use.

Display Typefaces

For authors, there are some considerations regarding typefaces:

- What are the required typefaces for companies and publishers?

- Which typefaces optimized for electronic books?

- Which typefaces can be used for electronic and paper books?

- What are the legal issues regarding the use of typefaces in a book?

Required Typefaces for Companies and Publishers

It is also a common practice for companies to use specific typefaces. For example, IBM uses a typeface family called IBM Bondoni, which is used in all its publications. This provides a consistent presentation of text in publications across the corporation. (IBM also requires specific typefaces and fonts to be used for all content displayed on its Internet and Intranet websites.)

If you are working with a publisher, the publisher may have a specific typeface that they expect you to use. Use of a specific typeface can provide a consistent presentation that is unique to that publisher. Other publishers may prefer the use of specific typefaces to make printing updates easier. For example, if you use Times Roman, which is a very common typeface, it is easier to match that typeface for printing as the printer will most likely have access to that typeface.

Recommended Typefaces for eBooks

As stated before, san-serif fonts are recommended for legibility. These san-serif fonts are recommended for consistent online display: Frutiger Linotype, Helvetica, and Verdana.

Both Adobe and Microsoft have developed fonts that are optimized for viewing online. Adobe offers these fonts: Caflisch

Script Web, Giddyup Web, Mezz Web, Minion, and Myriad. Microsoft offers: Andale Mono, Trebuchet, Georgia, Verdana, and Comic Sans. In general, the best method for determining which typefaces to use is to experiment and test using applications like Acrobat Reader and Microsoft Reader.

Recommended Font Sizes

Typically, fonts used in printed books range from 9 to 10 points in size and usually include a serif font, such as Times Roman. For electronic books, font sizes range from 11 to 13 points and they are usually san-serif fonts, such as Verdana. In addition, for electronic books, kerning should be avoided as while manipulating space between characters is fine and often desirable for print, kerning can produce unexpected results when viewed online.

A good compromise might be to use an 11 point font for the electronic and print versions as it is common to read business documentation in 12 point while 10 point is very common in the book industry. Some people, such as this author find 10 point somewhat limited for intensive reading, and perhaps for our poor, tired, eyes.

Another viewpoint, expressed by Coyne (2001), is that serif fonts will work fine, though many serif fonts, like Times Roman, are too thin while sans-serif fonts, such as Helvetica and Arial, are too thick. Coyne recommended the use of Century for serif and News Gothic for sans-serif (though Verdana is also recommended). For eBooks, Coyne recommended 12 point and Pirouz (2000) recommended a minimum point size of 14.

Typeface Technology: CoolType and ClearType

Adobe's CoolType and Microsoft's ClearType provide improved legibility of typefaces that are viewed on a Red Green Blue (RGB) matrix display or, more simply put, the kinds of computer displays you use with a laptop or personal display assistant or handheld computer. The importance of these tools is that it is much easier to read text on a computer display. The way this technology works is to control the intensity of the red, green, and blue pixels used in color displays to enhance legibility.

Though techniques like font smoothing have been used in the past, the technologies of CoolType and ClearType provide improvements that are easily seen. Both products offer users the ability to use, in essence, an eye chart to select a resolution that appears to be the easiest to read. This eye chart approach makes it easy to see how the reading experience is improved on laptops and handheld computers.

Legal Issues in Using Typefaces: Read the EULA

Unfortunately, technology, such as TrueType, has made typefaces very accessible to authors to include in their books, whether electronic or paper. Consider when you buy Corel Draw, not only does the product come with clip art, Corel Draw also comes with typefaces, which you can easily include in your book. However, do you have the right to use the typefaces in your book?

The answer is you have to read the End User License Agreement (EULA) that comes with the typefaces. (When you installed the product, you had to read the EULA as part of the process; you remember reading the EULA?)

Adobe (2000) provides this advice: "Embedding certain typefaces in Adobe PDF documents is legal, but readers cannot use those fonts in their own documents. In addition, readers may not edit documents with embedded typefaces unless those typefaces are licensed to and installed on the computer performing the editing. Typefaces in the Adobe Type Library that were created by Adobe, Linotype, ITC, Monotype, Agfa, and Fundicion Tipografica Neufville may be embedded in Adobe PDF documents for viewing and printing the document. Fonts from other companies may or may not be approved for embedding in Adobe PDF files."

Thomas Merz (1998) summed up this issue in *Web Publishing with Acrobat/PDF*, when he wrote: "The legitimacy of font embedding is not simply an issue of fairness to typographers: there is also the question of whether you want to take a legal risk with your publication. It is often hard to prove the origins of pirated software, but it's usually very easy to prove the originals of a PDF file from the Web – after all, a publisher generally wants to reach as many people as possible." And when you think about it, this is also an issue with electronic books: do you want someone copying or using part of your book without your permission or without compensation?

Font Fun?

If you are using "name brand" fonts, such as those provided with Adobe Type Manager, or Apple, or Microsoft TrueType, there are few restrictions and for other fonts, such as those provided by Bitstream and Corel, the license agreements can be easily read and understood. For fonts provided by other vendors, read the license agreement carefully.

Perfecting the eBook

One problem with using a particular typeface is if that typeface is not suited to both eBooks and pBooks, then you may/will have to create two versions of the book: one optimized for electronic display; one optimized for paper. If your publisher requires the use of Times Roman for the body of your book and another typeface, such as Helvetica, for headings, there may be problems with the eBook version. Because Times Roman is a serif font, it will be harder to read online. In that case, you might have to convert the body of the text to another typeface, like a san-serif font or a font that is optimized for viewing on a display, such as Verdana.

The reality is the ePublishing industry is still developing and you have to be prepared to publish more than one version of your book in paper and electronic format and probably more than one electronic version. For this book, a choice was made to publish a paper version and a version in Adobe Acrobat with selected chapters in other formats. One reason for this, is the number of tables contained in this book, would require, in this author's opinion, much rework to fit other formats. This is also an example of how genre effects the presentation of the material and how the material is written. Consider if this book did not present data on usability studies, then the use of tables would be minimal, and thus, easier to port to other formats. Therefore, as things are now, it is not a matter of perfecting the eBook but instead compromising to reach as many users as possible.

Part 2: ePublishing

"During the first century of printing the scribes who were practicing the art of natural writing and the printers practicing the new art of artificial writing competed for the same customers. The printing press did not [immediately] put the scribes out of business. Nearly as many manuscript books survive from the second half of the fifteenth century, after the invention of printing, as from the first half...For a while, there was enough business for both scribes and printers. But as the price of printed books declined, scribes began to have trouble finding work...As scribes saw the printed book was here to stay, they began to cooperate...[and] started using the press...by inserting printed sections into their manuscript books." Daniel J. Boorstin, *The Discoverers*, 1983.

Before ePublishing there has to be an eBook, Harold Henke, 2001

Part 2 is about electronic publishing. It begins by describing the importance of an odd sounding term, metadata, which is data that is needed to describe the electronic book. Then a description of Digital Rights Management is presented, the technology that is needed to protect the content of the electronic book from unauthorized use. The next few chapters describe changes to the publishing business from the author and publisher's view, as well, as the point of view of experts in the industry. After that, information is presented on the development of standards and on organizations that are active in providing information on the electronic book and publishing industry. Finally, some "how to" information is presented for authors who want to create their own electronic books using Microsoft Word and Adobe FrameMaker.

Chapter 5: Searching for Metadata

Creating an enjoyable consumer experience is a primary concern for publishers and authors of eBooks...this involves not only creating a quality product but creating accurate, detailed, descriptive product information – metadata – to help consumers locate [search for] desired titles and make informed decisions about acquiring [buying] them. Association of American Publishers, 2001

Metadata: What Is It?

Metadata is defined as descriptive data about data, which seems like a circular definition but metadata is really information which is included in the electronic book to describe the eBook content as well as ePublishing information, such as usage rules. Metadata in eBooks can include basic information, such as author, date published, number to identify book, to the data needed for search technology (keywords), to usage rights, to marketing information (such as royalty fees), and so on. Metadata is quite comprehensive and an area where standards are being developed to define a minimum set of metadata required to support ePublishing.

A simple way to think about metadata as it pertains to eBooks is as a book index. Consider that a typical book index is a list of terms that describes the content within the eBook. The list of terms is provided to enable a user to find information within the book. Additionally, by looking through an index, users can determine how well a particular subject is covered in the book or whether the subject is covered at all. In eBooks, metadata describes not only content but also information on terms and conditions, copyright information, version, format, territorial rights, and related information. Therefore, metadata is not intended solely for users but is also intended for use by authors, agents, publishers, distributors, and retailers.

What is the Importance of Metadata?

Metadata is important because users need a way to find information about your book and publishers and retailers need to provide information about the book for cataloguing and marketing. For authors, the inclusion of metadata can influence sales because metadata is necessary to help users find and buy your book.

Rust and Bide (2000) stated that "Metadata, as quoted from John Erickson [when employed by Yankee Trader, a Digital Rights Management provider], is the lifeblood of e-commerce" and that electronic trading requires much more information than traditional commerce, such as bricks and mortar, on how products are identified and the terms [metadata] in which the products are described. Consider when you shop at a bookstore (the bricks and mortar type); books are organized into categories, like history, and then arranged by author. You can crane your neck and search through each shelf and when you find a book that seems interesting, you can pull the book from the shelf and read the covers, browse the table of contents and index, or thumb through the book. If you do not find the book you need, you can ask the store personnel to search online and often the online search involves the use of keywords, like author name. Alternatively, the store personnel might be able to recommend a book or tell you that the bestselling book is out of stock.

Now consider searching for a book online. Currently, most searches are limited to keywords, titles, and author (just like the electronic searches done at the brick and mortar bookstores) but you cannot browse the shelves. Moreover, you cannot ask store personnel for recommendations. This is why metadata is important because with well-defined metadata (remember this is data about the eBook), users can search on a description of books, subject, price, number of illustrations, and a horde of other information. Better yet, this information can be cataloged and packaged so that you can search on a topic, such as Human-Computer Interaction, and get a collection of books that includes a package of information about each book.

An important aspect of metadata is what metadata belongs in an electronic book and who puts that information into the content?

Organizations like the Association of American Publishers, the EDItEUR, the Book Industry Communication, the Book Industry Study Group, the Electronic Book Exchange, and the Open Electronic Book Forum have all worked together and independently to define metadata for electronic books.

The reason so many organizations have weighed into this subject is that unless there are some standards, metadata that describes electronic books will be used helter-skelter and this may cripple the nascent industry. Here are some questions that illustrate how a helter-skelter use of metadata can impact the electronic book industry:

- How do you identify an electronic book? With paper books, an International Standard Book Number (ISBN) is assigned (if necessary, one for paperback; one for hardback) to the book. For electronic books, do you need to assign an ISBN for each format (hardback, paperback, electronic) and for specific electronic book formats, such as LIT, PDF, and REB? See Identifying eBooks: Will Any Name Do? for a detailed discussion on this topic.

- What subject categories should exist? If customers want to shop for an electronic book on history, would they search on a keyword like history, or European history, or 16th century European history? Consistent use of metadata will make it easier to catalog electronic books and make searching for electronic books more efficient.

- What metadata belongs in the electronic book? Metadata can encompass data about audience, prices, discounts, language, and so on. Is there a minimum set of data that should be included?

Where Metadata is Already Used

Before discussing the various types of metadata that may be included in an electronic book, here are some simple examples of how authors have already been using metadata.

Microsoft Word and Metadata

When you create a document in Microsoft Word, you create metadata based on the document's properties. For example, open a document in Microsoft Word, select **File**, then select **Properties**, and then **Summary**. The information contained in **Summary** is the metadata that is used by Microsoft Word to search for the document. (This information is also used by Adobe Acrobat and Microsoft Reader to supply metadata to electronic books.)

Even though this is a simple example of metadata, consider how many metadata elements are provided: title, subject, author, manager, company, category, keywords, and comments, and think about the amount of information about a book these elements can provide. Yet, if you look at a collection of Microsoft Word documents, you often find only metadata elements such as the author's name and the date created. Therefore, even though it is very easy to add metadata to Microsoft Word documents, authors often do not and that is because they are not aware of the usefulness of the metadata.

Acrobat and Metadata

When you create a PDF using Adobe Acrobat, you can also create similar metadata as with Microsoft Word. Open a PDF file and select **File**, then select **Document Information** and then select **General Information**. The metadata elements are: title, subject, author, keywords, creator, producer, created, and modified.

Most of these fields can be updated with content and authors can add very valuable metadata but, as is typical with Microsoft Word documents you often find only metadata elements such as author's name and title with complete information. Even though it is easy to add metadata to Acrobat documents, authors often do not because they are not aware of the usefulness of the metadata. What is also interesting is that when you use Adobe Acrobat Reader with Search, you can search on these fields and, with a large collection of PDF files, these fields can help users find a book or document quickly. Unfortunately, these fields are often blank, thus depriving users of the ability to conduct a meaningful search.

Metadata Standards: Three Key Sources

There are three key sources of metadata for ePublishing:

1. The Editeur – sponsored the Edituer Product Information Communication Standard (EPICS) and Online Information Exchange (ONIX). These standards were jointly developed by Edituer, Association of American Publishers, Book Industry Study Group, and Book Industry Communication.

2. The Association of American Publishers (AAP) – worked with Anderson Consulting to publish the *Metadata Standards for eBooks*.

3. The Open Electronic Book Forum – published some metadata information in the Publication Structure.

Edituer: EPICS and ONIX Metadata

Editeur (http://www.editeur.org) is an organization that developed and published the ONIX international standard that defines book product information for electronic commerce. Much of the current discussion on what metadata belongs in electronic books is derived from the ONIX standard. Another key activity from Editeur is the Editeur Product Information Communication Standards (EPICS) which is an international standard that provides a data dictionary, which is a list of defined metadata terms that can be used for ePublishing.

In this section, the focus will be on the efforts of the Association of American Publishers (AAP) and the Open Electronic Book Forum (OEBF) as these two organizations, who have pooled their efforts, are leading the way to define the metadata required specifically for eBooks.

Association of American Publishers: Metadata

The AAP published a proposed standard for metadata titled *Metadata Standards for Ebooks*. The document was published in conjunction with research conducted by Andersen Consulting and publishing companies. The AAP defined three types of metadata:

1. Discovery metadata, which can be considered, information needed to find eBooks, such as title, author, and abstract. This metadata would be used in catalogs (databases) used by retailers (such as those used to search for books on an online retailer).

2. Core metadata is a subset of the discovery metadata and is included with the eBook.

3. Private metadata is metadata that is used only by publishers, distributors, and retailers to facilitate ePublishing and is not available for use by users.

The AAP has recommended that the following "core metadata" elements be "bundled with the content [eBook] and delivered to the end user in the ePackage." (AAP, 2001). Note: a useful document to review to understand the following metadata is the *EPICS Data Dictionary* available from Editeur. In the AAP suggested standard, not all of these elements are considered crucial, some are "strongly suggested" while others are considered enhancements. In the following table, I make no distinctions as the more metadata, the more merrier the ePublishing business. Simply put, most of these elements are very useful and should be "strongly suggested" for all eBooks.

Metadata Element	Definition
Audience	United States school grades and interest ages. This can include many categories including: children, teenage or young adult, primary/secondary, tertiary education, professional and scholarly, and English as a second language.
Contributor and role	This is the author but can also include editor, illustrator, and others who "contributed" to the development of the eBook.
Currency	The monetary denomination in which the eBook is sold. For example, it is usual to see magazines, like the *Economist*, with prices listed for many countries, and this is the same concept for eBooks.
Edition	This is not only the traditional edition notice it can also contain fields which indicate whether the eBook: revised, abridged, annotated, illustrated, expurgated where offensive content has been removed, critical, and variorum, which means various commentators and critics have added information to the eBook.
File size	Total number of bytes of the eBook including all of the packaging information.
Illustrations	Number of illustrations in the eBook.
Images/audio/visual	Type and format of media included in the eBook. Also, defines what types of links are used, such as URL or FTP and so on.
Imprint	Imprint or brand name of the publisher.
Language	Text language and, if translated, then original language.

On sale date	This could be a range of dates for a sale or promotion that is tied into a Digital Rights Management system.
Other text	This is a very expansive category and can include material such as an abstract, flap cover, biographical note, descriptions for bookstores and libraries, and reviews by critics.
Pages	Number of pages in the eBook.
Prize	Description of any prizes awarded to the "contributor" or publisher of the eBook.
Product numbers	ISBN or Digital Object Identifier.
Publisher	Publisher and country of publication.
Publishing dates	Announcement date, publication date, year first published, year last published, and copyright date.
Referring ISBN	If the content of the eBook was originally published in another format, typically hard cover or paper back, then this field is used to tie the eBook version to the original paper version.
Retail price	Price, which can include a tax like Value Added Tax, and the actual selling price.
Series Information	Used if the eBook is part of a series. For example, an ISBN is used for the series, series title, number within the series, and year in annual.
Set information	Used if eBook is part of a set or collection and would include information such as volume number.
Subject	The subject can be derived from many sources, such as Book Industry Communication, Library of Congress, or even keywords derived from the person who created the metadata.
Territorial Rights	Country or region sales rights. For example, an eBook may not be for sale in a particular region or country and hence, this

	information would be added to the territorial rights.
Title and subtitle	Title and subtitle also includes an element for title prefix, which takes care of those definite and indefinite articles, that are included in many titles.
Website	Link to a website that is associated with the eBook, such as a publisher or author website.

Table 16: AAP Recommended Metadata

Open Electronic Book Forum: Metadata

The OEBF Publication Structure, Version 1.0.1, provides an understanding of and defines the requirements for metadata in electronic books. The OEBF has defined a book package as a collection of items that defines the electronic book. These items include: publication identity, metadata, manifest, spine, tours, and guide. For this section, the metadata requirements are described.

There are two types of metadata that can be included in an electronic book:

1. Metadata defined by the Dublin Core, which represents metadata derived from standards.

2. Metadata uniquely created for each electronic book, which represents metadata that is customized based on the author, publisher, distributor, and retailer requirements.

The OEBF recommended metadata that should be included in an electronic book package is based on work of the "Dublin Core Language" which was a consortium that defined metadata for information. The OEBF metadata is based on existing standards work and is applicable, world-wide. This is important for ePublishing because if the metadata elements are used consistently, then distributors and retailers will be able to catalog electronic books and thus provide more information to customers and manage inventories easier.

For example, if all authors and publishers include the description and subject metadata elements in their electronic books, then this information can be gleaned from each electronic book and presented to customers for viewing. Retailers and distributors will build applications that can extract this information for presentation to customers and thus they can easily create catalogs that include the description and subject information which represents an important element of the ePublishing infrastructure.

Here is a list of the key elements that the OEBF Publication Structure 1.0.1 recommends should be included in an electronic book. The only required metadata elements are: title and identifier. Typically, these metadata elements are included in the package file (an example is shown below) but these metadata elements can be included in the electronic book source files as well. (Note: a few metadata elements listed in the OEBF Publication Structure 1.0.1 have been omitted from this table as the definitions of the elements were not available. (A complete list is provided in the OEBF Publication Structure, 1.0.1.)

Metadata Element	Definition
Contributor	This is defined as the people who contributed to the publishing of the electronic book. Typically, examples used today would include illustrator and editor. The OEBF does require that specific formats be used, such as edit for editor and ill for illustrator.
Coverage	Place or time the book covers. This is a useful for textbooks,such as history books. The coverage element represents the concept that metadata elements can be used to provide much more information about a book than was available in the past.
Creator	Creator can include two useful attributes: 1) role which is based on the attributes described under contributor, such as author and 2) file-as, which is useful for "card cataloging" authors such as file-as: Henke, Harold A.

Date	Date based on W3 organization's recommended date structure: YYYYMMDD (Only the year is required). There is also an optional event attribute which can be used for providing additional dates, such as date camera-ready-copy was provided to the publisher. For date and event, these are determined by the author, publisher, and there are no exact rules. You would expect traditional use of dates, like the copyright date and printing history (assuming the book is available in both electronic and paper format) to be used with date and event.
Description	Typically would include the information found on the "dust jacket" or could even be a reviewer's review of the book.
Identifier	A required element that identifies the electronic book. How to identify electronic books is an issue that will require attention from the publishing community as there are many schemes currently available but, in any event, each electronic book must include this element. See Identifying eBooks: Will Any Name Do? for a discussion on this issue.
Language	Identifies the languages used to present the content.
Publisher	This is the book publisher.
Rights	This metadata element can be very simple or very complex. From a simple perspective, this element contains the copyright notice, and from a complex perspective, this element contains information about the Digital Rights Management system used to protect the electronic book.
Source	If parts of the book were derived from a previous book, the source is listed here. An example might be an anthology with multiple sources.
Subject	Can be a collection of keywords or a specific phrase. This is an area where you need both a

	set of keywords agreed upon by the industry as well as the freedom to include any words or phrases that would help catalogue the electronic book to make it easier for users to find and for retailers to distribute.
Title	Publication title
Type	Can be a way to catalog the content, such as poem, reference, dictionary, and so on. This is an area where you need both a set of types agreed upon by the industry as well as the freedom to include any words or phrases that would help catalogue the electronic book to make it easier for users to find and for retailers to distribute.

Table 17: OEBF Recommended Metadata

Example of Standard Metadata in OEBF Package

Here is an example of the markup language adapted from the OEBF Publication Specification 1.0.1, where dc is Dublin Core. The point of this illustration is simply that entering metadata is easy and authors should be prepared to add metadata to their electronic books or at least expect their publisher to do so.

```
<package unique-identifier="xyz">
<metadata>
<dc-metadata
xmlns:dc="http://purl.org/dc/elements/1.0/"
xmlns:oebpackage="http://openebook.org/namespaces/o
eb-package/1.0/">
<dc:Title>eBooks and ePublishing</dc:Title>
<dc:Type>Reference</dc:Type>
<dc:Identifier id="xyz"
scheme="ISBN">123456789X</dc:Identifier>
<dc:Creator role="aut">Harold A. Henke</dc:Creator>
</dc-metadata>
</metadata>
 </package>
```

Figure 3: An Example of Standard Metadata Markup

Custom Metadata

In addition to metadata elements defined by the Dublin Core, the OEBF Publication Structure, 1.0.1, also recognizes that authors, publishers, and retailers will need to create their own metadata elements. For example, a metadata element that will probably be quite common is price. Other possible custom metadata might include:

- The number of pages, illustrations, or tables (useful information for reference books)

- Price information like the retail selling price.

- The expiration date for documents that have a set life and expire after a certain time. For example, some standards like ISO 14001, dictate that if a procedure or document is not updated after a certain period, it expires.

Example of Custom Metadata in the OEBF Package

Here is an example of the custom metadata markup adapted from the OEBF Publication Specification 1.0.1. The point of this illustration is simply that entering metadata is easy and authors should be prepared to add metadata to their electronic books or at least expect their publisher to do so.

```
<metadata>
<dc-metadata>
</dc-metadata>
<x-metadata>
<meta name="price" content="USD 29.99"/>
</x-metadata>
</metadata>
```

Figure 4: Example of Custom Metadata

Identifying eBooks: Will Any Name Do?

Currently no agreed upon standard exists on how to identify the electronic book. With paper books, most published books use an ISBN to identify the book (if there are hardcover and paperback versions, then each version is assigned a ISBN). For magazines, the International Standard Serial Number (ISSN) is assigned. Nevertheless, for electronic books, you may need a separate number for each format, like LIT, PDF, or REB formats.

This presents a huge problem: how do retailers and librarians catalog a book with no unique number or multiple numbers? Is the answer to continue using ISBN, or is a European Article Number or Universal Product Code (bar codes) the answer? Or shoulld we use something called a Digital Object Identifier (DOI), which is a number assigned only to digital content, such as an eBook? The AAP has made recommendations in the *Numbering Standard for Ebooks* (2001) on this subject, which includes:

- Implement an identification system based on using a DOI as defined by the International DOI Foundation.

- Assign an ISBN and DOI for each eBook and pBook. The AAP states that one DOI should be used for all formats of the eBook (which means if the eBook was available in LIT and PDF, only one DOI would be issued for the two formats).

- Use a DOI identification structure that includes a prefix that identifies the organization that registered the eBook, and a suffix that is provided by the organization and could be, for example, ISBN.

Some of the implications of the AAP's proposed naming system is that there would need to be an organization that could register part of the information needed for the DOI, which is the prefix part, and that organizations like publishers would need to use the suffix consistently. In the near term, authors and publishers are most likely going to assign an ISBN for each type of eBook and pBook or perhaps, no number at all for eBooks.

The Metadata ePublishing Highway

The definition of what metadata is and the consistent use of metadata is crucial to the ePublishing infrastructure. If you think of ePublishing as a highway that enables electronic books to be distributed and sold, then metadata would be the highway signs that guide you on the highway. Without consistent use and definitions of metadata, users will be lost on the ePublishing highway.

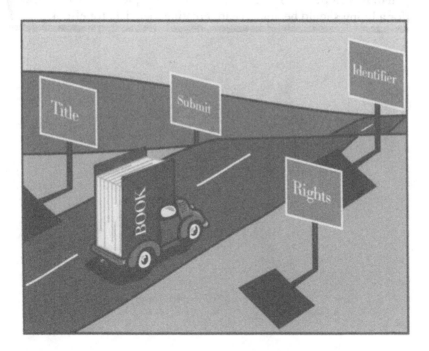

Figure 5: ePublishing Highway and Metadata

Metadata Money

For those entrepreneurs looking to participate in the ePublishing industry, and for authors, consider the fact that most published books have very little metadata available when previously published books are converted into electronic format, someone will need to add metadata to the content, for a price. Authors should be aware that their publishers might expect them to add the metadata to their books as part of the authoring process. Perhaps the biggest windfall will be for "indexers", that is, by people who index books for a living should be able to earn creating metadata for eBooks.

Chapter 6: Protecting Content in a Digital Age

"As piracy makes the cost of information fall toward zero, its obtainability becomes inversely proportional to its value. Infinite access = infinite mess." Charles C. Mann, 2000

Digital Rights Management

In addition to protecting your intellectual rights, as an author, you also want to protect your right to royalties and you want your users to be able to perform tasks like loan the book to their friends so they can preview your book and then buy their own copy. These goals are accomplished through the application of Digital Rights Management technology to electronic books.

The subject of Digital Rights Management (DRM) is complex and worthy of its own book, thus, the intent of this chapter is to provide authors with a fundamental understanding of DRM. Authors may wonder what DRM means to them so here are some questions that underscore issues associated with distribution and use of electronic books:

- How will publishers keep track of the number of books sold? For paper books, the process is well defined but how do you count electronic books? Can you go to the bookstore and check the inventory?

- Can my work be protected from being changed or altered? With a paper book, it is hard to alter the book after it is printed but can the electronic book be altered after it is distributed? Will two versions exist for the same electronic book?

- Will it be easier to plagiarize my work if it is in an electronic format? Can someone simply copy entire sections of my book?

- Can users loan my book to other users? Is there a way to send out preview copies to reviewers?

Definition of Digital Rights Management

DRM can be defined in two parts:

1. Protection via encryption to prevent unauthorized copying;

2. Rights management that can be defined as enforcement of usage rules.

Usage rules include tasks such as whether a user can print the book or loan the book to another user, to more esoteric tasks such as setting a sales price with a begin and end date. Though there is more focus on copy protection through encryption, managing the usage rules is equally important for the author, publisher, and users.

The simplest way to understand DRM is to relate it to tasks or usage rules that are typically applied to paper books. For example, a simple rule would be to prevent users from making copies of an electronic book and a more complex usage rule would be to enable, or not enable, users to resell their electronic book (like they might do with their previously read paper book).

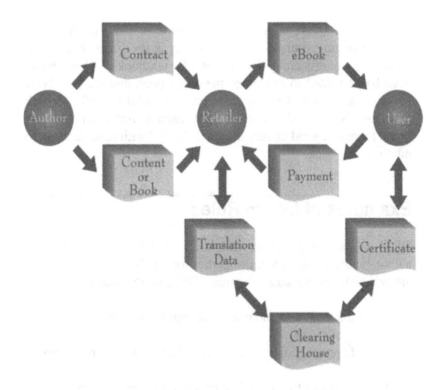

Figure 6: DRM Scenario

Usage Rules for Real World Tasks

An interesting aspect of DRM is that while the fear of piracy is a real fear and protection from piracy is the driving force for developing DRM systems, there are advantages provided by DRM systems that enable tasks to be performed with electronic books that are not possible with paper books. If you are an author who writes textbooks, users could get a trial version of the book, and decide to buy the book after the trial. Alternatively, users could "sample" a chapter or browse the table of contents.

With paper books, unless a user can find the book in a bookstore or library, or maybe read a description on a website, it is very difficult to preview a book. The likelihood is the user would have to wait until their local library obtained a copy before they could "try and buy". With DRM, the possibilities of enabling users to view your book, either the whole book or parts of the book, while protecting your book from copying is great and should help expand sales, especially for genres like textbooks. Users could even be permitted to download the entire book and read the book for a week or two. This "try and buy" or "trial bomb" approach promotes "stickiness" or, simply put, once a user downloads the book, there is a good chance they will "stick" with their decision to purchase the book.

Examples of Usage Rules

DRM is best thought of as what kinds of tasks or usage rules do authors and publishers want to permit for an electronic book. Here are typical tasks or usage rules that a DRM system can enforce:

- Keep track of sales and users who purchase the book.

- Provide review copies with limited distribution for reviewers.

- Enable the electronic book to be loaned to another user.

- Enable users to replace a book that has been deleted.

- Permit or prohibit printing.

- Permit, or prohibit, copying of parts of the book

- Provide, try and buy, or trial bomb which is a free preview of a book that has a start and end date.

- Permit or prohibit the book from being resold.

- Permit or prohibit the book from being donated.

- Enable the book to be read (or moved from one device to another device) on a variety of devices.

- Embed watermarks to track usage.

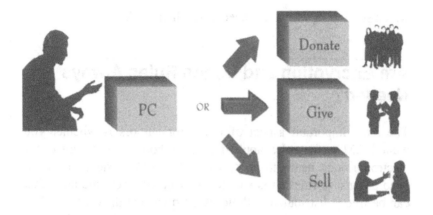

Figure 7: Examples of Usage Rules

Example of Everyday Use of DRM Technology

If you have created an Acrobat PDF file using Adobe Acrobat, you have already created usage rules and used a form of DRM technology. When you create a PDF file, you can set these security options from Acrobat Distiller, which represent the two aspects of DRM, encryption and rights management, which are described below:

- A password to open the document and a password to change the security levels (a form of DRM encryption to prevent unauthorized use).

- Enable or not enable printing (a usage rule to prevent printing).

- Changing the document (a usage rule to prevent modifications).

- Selecting text and graphics (a usage rule to prevent cut and paste).

- Adding or changing notes or form fields.

The above examples are simple in nature but provide good examples of how an author can apply DRM technology to their book. The real issue for authors is what level of protection and which set of usage rules are needed for their books.

Are Encryption and Usage Rules Always Needed?

The most important aspect of DRM for authors is whether you want DRM usage rules applied to your book or not. Not every electronic book needs to be protected by DRM systems nor even need any usage rules. It is simple to create an electronic book that can be freely distributed with no usage rules. On the other hand, if you are writing a textbook for a publisher, you can expect that your book will include usage rules.

If you have signed a contract with a publisher and you are going to publish an electronic book, then you will not have to consider whether you need encryption or usage rules because the publisher will need outlets to distribute the book and encryption and usage rules will be applied. The author's role in that case is quite limited (other than to review their contract and check the electronic rights section <grin>).

If you are publishing your electronic book on your own or using one of the self-publishers (also called, by some, vanity publishers), you will want to consider what level of security and what usage rules you want to apply.

Consider the business model you intend to use to publish your book and then consider how important it is for you to prevent unauthorized usage. Some business models are simply based on securing payment for the electronic book, just the same as buying a paper book. If that is your business model, then you probably do not want nor need much security.

For example, when you create an electronic book in Microsoft's LIT format, Microsoft states that when you convert content to the Microsoft LIT format, the content is "sealed" or encrypted which represents the "basic level of security given to each .lit file" (Microsoft, 2000). This means your electronic book in Microsoft LIT format is protected from being modified.

> ## Suggestion
>
> If you are considering publishing your electronic book yourself, the use of a publisher, who can manage the security and usage of your book, is highly recommended. Unless your business model is to sell your books at a price that discourages theft, then you will want to use some sort of DRM technology to manage encryption and usage rules. Additionally, not only do you want to protect your book against theft, you want to ensure that your ideas and the way you expressed them, are also protected, in essence, in a tamper-proof package.

DRM: Issues

Though, as stated at the beginning of this chapter, this is not a book on DRM there are issues that effect authors and users, and if these issues are not resolved, the eBook industry may falter. The key issues are:

- Reversion of Rights to the author.

- Privacy.

- Super Distribution.

Reversion of Rights to the Author

Most publishing agreements include a clause that if a paper book goes out-of-print, the author can request that the rights to the book revert back to the author so the author can offer the book to another publisher or publish the book themselves. With an electronic book (and print-on-demand books) the book never goes out-of-print, so does this mean the rights never revert to the author? This is not as much a technology issue that needs to be solved but more a business issue that needs to be resolved between authors, literary agents, and publishers. (Check your contract and make sure electronic rights are defined!)

User Privacy

When you buy a paper book in a bookstore, you can pay for the book and, more often than not, the fact you bought a particular book is not recorded. (Though this is not true with online booksellers who offer you the "convenience" of tracking the types of books you like to read.) However, with the purchase of an electronic book, information must be exchanged between the buyer and seller and this information can easily be recorded and passed on to third parties.

Emerging technologies, for example digital fingerprinting and watermarking, which are needed to combat piracy, are used to store information about the user who purchased the book. However, this information can be stored by the seller and thus the seller can build a database of users and their reading habits quite quickly. Simply put, it may be possible that the reading habits of electronic book users will be easily captured, stored, and used for marketing.

While there is much debate about privacy on the Internet, the privacy of what you read in your home is an explosive issue. Gervais (1998) stated that scholars in the United States have argued that the United States Constitution "protects a right to read anonymously". If users believe that each time they buy an electronic book, about them information is embedded in the book and in the seller's database, users may choose not to buy electronic books at all for fear of being marketed to death.

With regards to user privacy, DRM technology can provide protection to users as well as gather user information. The work of groups like the AAP and the OEBF will help develop standards that define what DRM is and help define privacy policies. Thus, user privacy, is as much a DRM technology issue, as a cultural issue.

Super Distribution

Super distribution is an ugly term that encompasses tasks that users will want to do with their electronic book. Specifically, users will want to:

- Buy a book as a gift for another user.

- Read a book and then resell the book to a used book dealer.

- Read a book and then donate the book to a library or give the book to a friend.

If a book is "licensed" to one user, the DRM technology will need to enable users to perform the tasks listed above. If not, then the use of an electronic book by users will be much more constrained than a paper book. Nevertheless, as with privacy, these issues need to be sorted out by organizations like the AAP and the OEBF.

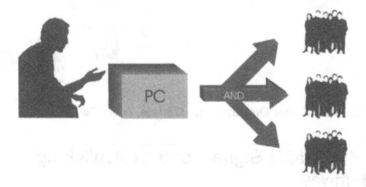

Figure 8: Super Distribution - Sending a Book to Many Users

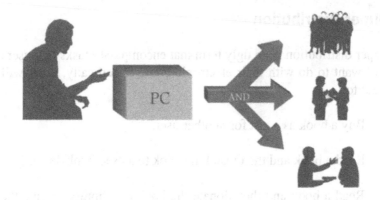

Figure 9: Super Distribution - One to Many Users

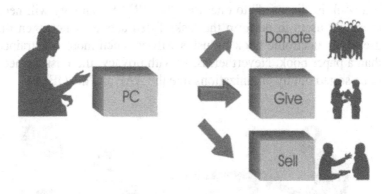

Figure 10: Super Distribution - Donate, Give, Sell

DRM: Traffic Signals of the ePublishing Highway

On one level, DRM is not the author's concern as usually the encryption and usage rules will be meshed out between the publisher and distributor; on the other level, if the author is publishing their own work, or perhaps through a vanity imprint, then the author will be more involved in deciding what level of security is needed and what usage rules are necessary.

Whether author or publisher, DRM is important to enabling ePublishing. If metadata represents the signs that guide consumers to find eBooks, then DRM represents the traffic signals on the ePublishing highway. Without a method to protect content, the value of content will become zero. However, a system cannot be used that prevents users from using an eBook in a manner they consider fair and that matches their expectations of how they use a pBook. Thus, implementation of DRM technology is an issue of technology but also an issue of culture and requires not only industry cooperation but also consumer support.

DRM Resources

Here are additional resources for information on DRM issues. From these resources, you can find information about other organizations that are active in DRM technology issues.

Association of American Publishers

The AAP has provided leadership to the publishing community by working with Anderson Consulting to define requirements for standards for DRM, publication numbering systems, and metadata. In addition to the AAP, publishers like Random House, McGraw-Hill, and Pearson have also participated in the AAP project. The report, *Reading in the New Millennium, A Bright Future for eBook Publishing: Facilitated Open Standards*, was published jointly by Anderson Consulting and the AAP and you can read about potential markets for electronic books and a description of DRM. You can find *Reading in the New Millennium* and other reports on DRM and other issues on the AAP website, www.publishers.org.

Copyright Clearance Center

The copyright clearance center provides a system to manage copyrights so that organizations like universities can obtain clearance to use copyrighted material for use such as photocopying articles for classroom use. From the Copyright Clearance Center, you can also obtain information on the International Federation of Reproduction Rights Organizations (IFRRO). The IFRRO is an umbrella organization for organizations that provide copyright management services. You can find articles on DRM and copyright issues for electronic books at the Copyright Clearance Center.

Open Electronic Book Forum

The OEBF published *A Framework for the ePublishing Ecology* by the OEBF DRM Working Group. The report provides an excellent glossary and a list of "stakeholders" or people who have a role in the electronic publishing process and who are affected by the use of DRM technology. In addition to the glossary and stakeholder definitions, the report also provides a description of the publishing process as it pertains to DRM. You can find the report and information on DRM at www.openebook.org.

Chapter 7: A New Print Economy?

"Yes, young people need 2 b educated that artists should be compensated 4 their work. But they don't need 2 b educated about how 2 hypocritically xploit artists by forcing them 2 participate in a system designed 2 sell products instead of sharing good music...online distribution might enable artists 2 put an end 2 this exploitation. And, by the looks of things, this will happen without the help or understanding of record company executives." Prince as quoted in Industry Standard, 2000

Traditional Publishing: Old Economy?

As companies were created to sell pet food and toys online via the Internet, along with many other companies that offered new services such as online bartering of goods, money (in the form of venture capital and initial public offerings), particularly in the United States equity market, flowed into these businesses. The media (newspaper, magazines, and television) began touting a new economy that did not rely on "bricks and mortar" to operate but relied on business to customer (B2C) or business to business (B2B) relationships. Some of these new businesses prospered, some very successfully, such as online booksellers. Others flourished until capital, supplied by venture capitalists and the equity markets, dried up, and many of these B2C and B2B companies found they could no longer support the cash flow required to fund their business models. Simply put, they spent more money than they made and, given how they made money, it was unlikely this scenario would change.

From the "dot.com" meltdown, investors and the media began to recognize that old economy companies have been spending capital to use the World Wide Web as part of their existing business models. In some cases, these old economy companies used the World Wide Web to facilitate communication between their companies and their suppliers (B2B) and to sell directly to their customers (B2C). Furthermore, some of the old economy companies began to tie their bricks and mortar infrastructure to their World Wide Web infrastructure to provide customers with the best of both worlds. (For example, some retailers will sell you a product online, such as a DVD title, and if you want to return the product, you can take it to the local "brick and mortar" store for a credit, thus eliminating the difficulty of sending product back via the World Wide Web.)

While this new economy was being formed, some of the traditional publishers moved to embrace the new economy and some of the "dot.coms" met the old economy.

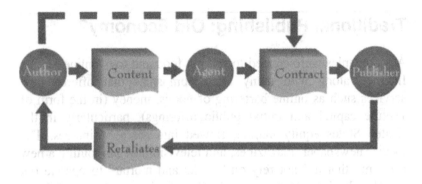

Figure 11: Traditional Publishing Model

Old Economy Meets New Economy

In the publishing industry, "old economy" publishers, like Random House and Time Warner, have adapted to the new economy and created imprints dedicated to eBooks and ePublishing.

Time Warner

Time Warner created an eBook publishing business called iPublish.com that will distribute and sell fiction and non-fiction via the World Wide Web. iPublish will not only include established Time Warner authors but new authors who may publish solely via iPublish.

Random House

Random House has moved into the new economy in two ways:

1. It has invested in Xlibris which helps authors to publish books and provides print on demand (books-on-demand) services. In essence, Xlibris provides authors with services used to "self-publish" their eBooks and pBooks. Therefore, Random House has invested in two profitable segments of ePublishing: self-publishing and print on demand (books on demand).

2. AtRandom is Random House's electronic book imprint that publishes only eBooks for first-time authors and established authors.

New Economy Meets Old Economy

While the traditional publishers were moving into the new economy, businesses solely dedicated to eBooks and ePublishing were being forced to retrench or change their business models. A couple of examples are:

iBooks

iBooks, which originally focused on selling eBooks to consumers, had to retrench when the company came to the conclusion that the original business model of converting content and selling the content to consumers was unsustainable. The Chief Executive Officer, George Leppert, stated: "I had undertaken an exhaustive analysis of the company from when I first came to the company [and] it was established in the publishing arena and was an elegant solution, but still it drew no traffic. This is a tough market to bust." Bartlett (2001)

iBooks has changed its business model to focus solely on providing digital information to businesses and government organizations, which is often referred to as business to business (B2B).

Fatbrain and MightyWords

Fatbrain's original business model was to enable authors to sell content, from articles to books, at any price the author wanted to sell. The purpose of Fatbrain was to enable authors to publish their content by simply renting space on Fatbrain's server and using Fatbrain to manage the business (eCommerce) aspects, such as paying for and downloading content. The original business model did not work well because consumers were leery of buying content from a site where articles ranged in price from $1.00 to $50.00. It was very hard for consumers to differentiate good content from bad content. In other words, if the content is priced low, then is any of the content valuable? The closer the value of the content is to free, the more likely the content is devalued.

But Fatbrain did not completely change its business model when MightyWords was launched, instead the company changed the focus of content by focusing on business, technical/computer, and health titles and by providing branded titles, in other words, content like eBooks from recognized authors or experts in the field (Kirkpatrick, 2000). This made Fatbrain/MightyWords function more like a publisher than a clearing house as MightyWords became selective about the content they sold to users via the World Wide Web. They now provide the function of "filtering" content so that users are assured that the content they buy has some brand value associated with it. (Note: Barnes and Noble purchased Fatbrain and owns 50 percent of MightyWords. Consolidation is a fact of live in the ePublishing world.)

Old Economy: New Economy or Hybrid?

An example of where the old economy has met the new economy and created a hybrid economy is in the way books are sold. Certainly, the World Wide Web has changed the way books are sold. At BookExpo America 2000, Jeff Bezos, founder of Amazon, spoke at the exhibition, which was tacit acknowledgement that the World Wide Web had changed, forever, how books were sold. Yet, BookExpo America has often been where members of the American Booksellers Association (ABA), which is comprised primarily of independent booksellers, have met to further their business. (Independent booksellers must believe that the fates are against them given the competition provided by "megastores" and now the World Wide Web with mega-virtual stores.)

At the BookExpo America 2000 conference, Richard Howarth, President of the ABA, stated, "...I think most people see that he [Bezos] reflects some of the changes in the book industry" (Italie, 2000a). In addition, at BookExpo, there were many presentations on eBooks and ePublishing, which, according to people who attended, was standing room only.

Though it is clear that the way books are sold has been changed dramatically by the World Wide Web, what is not so clear, at least yet, is what changes are in store for publishers and retailers. Consider that some book retailers only sell via the World Wide Web and have no "bricks and mortar" infrastructure whereas other retailers combine both World Wide Web and "bricks and mortar". Both models seem to work, though profitability seems to favor those companies that enable customers to buy books online or in person and to return (though, as authors, we know that return is a bad word) the book for a credit at their local "brick and mortar" store. Also, consider that some retailers seem also to be publishers and some publishers seem to be retailers. (While you have always been able to buy books from many publishers directly, the World Wide Web enables publishers to reach far larger markets than they could in the past. Direct sales are much simpler given a presence on the World Wide Web.)

The terms old and new economy do not make much sense for the publishing world, instead, what is important, is what business model will support making profit when publishing and selling eBooks and pBooks. Therefore, what publishing models will emerge for both publishers and retailers that support profitability? Is how business is conducted today, the model for tomorrow?

Future Publishing Models

Mandel (2000) reviewed a report by Forrester Research Incorporated that predicted three distribution models for eBooks and, for this book, a fourth model, based on subscription, has been added by this author.

Model	Description
Prevention	The eBook is encrypted and when a user buys the eBook, the eBook is decrypted. This is the current model that most publishers and retailers support and is the basis for most DRM systems. This model assumes that DRM technology can prevent widespread theft and that encryption keys can be protected from hackers. Also, if you consider that one of the arguments used for trading music files is that the "middleman" keeps most of the profits, not the artists, there will be a backlash against paying for eBooks.
Advertisement	The eBook is packaged with advertisements that the user must read as part of the eBook. Publishers make money by selling advertisement space and users buy the book at a discounted price or for free. This has been the model used for many "dot.com" companies but unfortunately; this model has not provided sustainable profits.
Marketplace	The eBook is sold through a clearing house where users can buy the eBook and trade it to another user who pays a fee for reading the eBook to the clearing house.
Subscription	The eBook is sold through a clearing house or the publisher in the form of a subscription. Users pay for a series of books or for chapters of a book. This is analogous to how software is sold to corporations today.

Table 18: Four Publishing Models

Prevention Publishing Model

This is the current model that most publishers and retailers support and it is the basis for most DRM systems. This model assumes that DRM technology can prevent widespread theft and that encryption keys can be protected from hackers. Also, if you consider that one of the arguments used for trading music files is that the "middleman" keeps most of the profits, not the artists, there will be a backlash against paying for eBooks.

Advantages:

- A straightforward business model; a user buys the eBook and is entitled to use the eBook as defined by the usage rules.

- There is support for this model within the publishing industry from authors, publishers, and retailers.

Disadvantages:

- It requires an infrastructure of clearing houses and tools to encrypt and decrypt the eBook, which adds costs to the eBook.

- If users cannot use an eBook in the same way they can use a pBook, such as loan the book to a friend or donate the eBook to a library, they will resist buying eBooks. The prevention model must support these tasks and these tasks must be simple for the user to complete.

Advertisement Publishing Model

Publishers make money by selling advertisement space and users buy the book at a discounted price or for free. This has been the model used for many "dot.com" companies but this model has not provided sustainable profits.

Advantages:

- Advertisements could be targeted to specific consumer groups and their associated demographics, such as science fiction readers. Unlike websites, which typically only track the number of users who visit the site, advertisements in eBooks could reach a targeted audience so advertisers would have more assurance that their advertisements were reaching the right audience.

- Users could send an eBook to another user with the condition that the user would have to go through each advertisement during the reading process. This would enable super distribution of eBooks by simply requiring that users who had not paid for the book would be required to read each advertisement as part of the price for receiving the free book.

Disadvantages:

- This model could be implemented in pBooks but has not been which suggests that users do not want advertisements in their eBooks. If such a model were implemented, would the eBook be provided free as a price for reading the advertisements? Could this model support a user who chooses to pay a higher price not to view advertisements?

- Can the technology support frequent updates of the advertisements? An eBook may be sold for many years; would the advertisements be out of date in months?

- Who controls the advertisements that are included in the eBook? Does the author have any input? Would the author of a children's book want advertisements for video games included in the eBook?

Marketplace Publishing Model

The marketplace model is based on the experiences of the music industry. In that case, users wanted a simple method to trade music and thus companies were created to facilitate music trading via the World Wide Web. Eventually, after many lawsuits, these businesses reached agreements with music publishers to pay royalties to enable users to trade music from their websites.

This model may work for eBooks as publishers could license eBooks to the companies, who would act as clearing houses so that each time a user downloaded a book, the user would pay a fee to the clearing house and that fee would be reported to the publisher. Users could receive a credit for uploading a book to the clearing house. Another offshoot of this model could be the renting of eBooks; in essence, the clearing houses could function as libraries. Users could rent an eBook for a specified time and the clearing house would be paid a rental fee that would be reported to the publisher.

Advantages:

- It fits the model that has been developed based on electronic distribution in the music industry. It may better fit the consumer who believes that electronic content, whether music or text, should be readily available and for a reasonable price which for some means free.

- It enables users to act as marketing representatives. Instead of just word of mouth, users would be encouraged to download eBooks by other users.

Disadvantages:

- It requires an infrastructure of clearing houses and tools to keep track of downloads.

- In the music industry, most popular (or newly released) music carries the same list price but with eBooks, the price has traditionally been set by factors like print costs and genre. A fiction novel is priced differently than a textbook. Either all eBooks will need to be priced similarly or the publishing model will need to be able to handle many different price points. This will be much more complicated than what is currently implemented in the music business.

- The music industry model is based on the premise that users do not want to pay for content (or at least they do not want to pay for content if they believe their favorite artist is not going to profit) and thus the best that can be achieved is some payment as opposed to no payment. Given the effort to write a book, the majority of authors will reject the notion that getting any payment for their work is better than no payment.

Subscription Publishing Model

This is analogous to how software is sold to corporations today. Instead of buying a specific upgrade to a product, corporations pay to get updates on a regular basis. The same business model may be applied to eBooks. For example, users may pay for a series of eBooks based on a genre, like science fiction. Other subscription models may be to buy chapters at a time which perhaps harks back to a time when pBooks were serialized and readers bought chapters at a time.

Advantages:

- Publishers would obtain a steady payment (in essence an annuity) for an eBook.

- Users could pay a subscription fee that would provide access to more publications than a typical single book sale.

Disadvantages:

- Given the immediacy of the World Wide Web, it is unlikely that users will want to wait for chapters to be available on a given timetable. This approach was more or less tried with a fiction novel by a well-known author but sales declined and part of this decline can be attributed to impatience on the part of the users waiting for the next chapter to be made available for download.

- Most subscription models would require users to pay money upfront for a subscription (or really a right to access content on a fixed schedule) and users typically do not like this approach. This works for corporations who buy software equally, and for magazines, but this approach has not been used since pBooks were serialized.

Penguins: Polar Bears or Killer Whales?

Publishers are facing a fundamental change to their business, called ePublishing, and the majority of them are acting very much like a Penguin standing on the edge of an ice shelf. Behind the penguin are polar bears (authors) who want to publish directly via the World Wide Web, and in front of the penguins are killer whales (users) who do not want to pay for any electronic content let alone eBooks. The publishers are not sure which predator represents the gravest danger to their business and thus, many publishers are frozen, waiting to see what happens.

Future Publishing: Author-Server-User Model

Richard Curtis, founder of eRights, described a new model of publishing at the 1999 National Institute of Standard and Technology conference, *Electronic Books: The Next Chapter.* He described a fundamental shift of power from publishers to authors as authors can take advantage of the Internet to distribute their work without relying on traditional publishers and their distribution channels. Curtis defined this new business model as author-server-user.

Curtis stated that the traditional publishing model encourages waste since 50% of all trade books are returned (remaindered) to the publishers for credit, which leads to low profit margins and to focusing on successful authors and relying less on finding the next great novelist (Curtis, 1999). Curtis believed that a new model, which he referred to as "authorcentric" was emerging where authors on their own or with help from service providers, could replace the publisher by performing the three most important tasks of a publisher: 1) print; 2) distribute; and 3) advertise (Curtis, 1999).

Curtis also stated that the author-server-user model has legitimatised self-publishing or vanity publishing and now makes it feasible to make a profit on a few hundred copies, which empowers a single author to publish their book, even if they only need to reach a very small or targeted audience. Curtis believed this revolution would be the "dot.communistic" of the publishing industry (Curtis, 2000).

Below is an illustration that shows the choices an author now has. Consider that an author can publish the eBook or pBook on his or her own (personal publishing) or with the help of a subsidy or vanity publishing company, or even with the help of a traditional publisher who has an imprint dedicated to ePublishing:

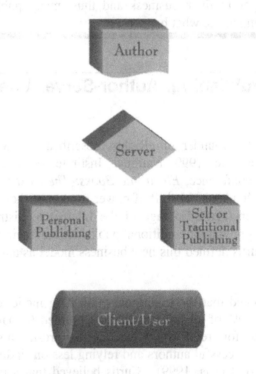

Figure 12: Author-Server-User

Future Publishing: Personal and Subsidy

As Curtis noted, ePublishing has made personal publishing and subsidy or vanity publishing legitimate. Rossiter-Modeland (2000) stated, "The stigma that was once attached to self-published paper books is eroding in self-published eBooks. Now that it is physically and financially possible for a writer to publish his or her own work and reap ALL the profits, more are doing so".

Subsidy Publishing: eStigma?

Though some in the industry believe that authors are becoming empowered by ePublishing, there is still a lingering distain for subsidy or vanity publishing. Rossiter-Modeland (2000) wrote, "Subsidy publishing in the print world...is highly stigmatized and unacceptable to writer's organizations, reviewers, distributors, and knowledgeable readers. Indications this negativity is carrying over into ePublishing...experienced authors and their organizations still frown on subsidy publishing because it is possible for anyone to pay to publish a book, regardless of quality". Yet, the fact that any author, known or unknown, can now easily publish a book does not guarantee any better work than those books published by subsidy or vanity publishers. Subsidy or vanity publishing is now mainstream in ePublishing and the real issue is how will users be able to sort the wheat from the chaff?

Though these forms or models of publishing have been around for a long time, the World Wide Web is providing authors with the ability to successfully publish eBooks and pBooks.

- With eBooks and pBooks that are printed using print on demand (books on demand), the fixed costs are limited and thus authors can quickly begin to make a profit. The infrastructure is in place for authors to manage their own websites to sell eBooks and pBooks or to contract a company to manage the ePublishing activities for them.

- There are no returns or remaindered copies; since eBooks and pBooks are sold on a per customer basis, the books are not returned. Curtis referred to this as "100% sell through as every copy that is sold, stays sold" (Curtis, 2000).

- The World Wide Web provides lower marketing costs as it is less expensive to market eBooks. There are user groups and websites devoted to communities of users that can be targeted for marketing activities.

- Established authors with a catalog of books can republish their books directly and gain incremental sales that would not have been possible with their previous publisher.

- Authors can establish their own communities of readers with whom they can interact directly. While book signings are quite interactive, they are limited in scope whereas the World Wide Web provides the author with a virtual, 24 by 7, book signing.

Definitions of Personal and Subsidy Publishing

Once an author has created the content for an eBook, there are many distribution channels available for publishing. Each channel defines how the author's content is packaged for distribution. Here are some definitions of these channels:

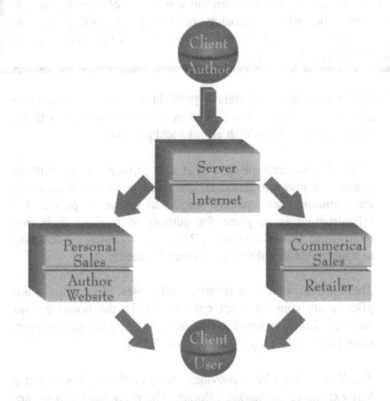

Figure 13: Client/Server Personal/Traditional Publishing

Personal Publishing

Personal publishing is defined as an author publishing an electronic book without using a publisher, service provider, or retailer. As was noted in Chapter 6: Protecting Content in a Digital Age, not every electronic book needs to be protected by DRM technology and not every electronic book needs to be sold through a publisher or retailer.

To differentiate personal publishing from self or vanity publishing, here are some attributes of personal publishing:

- Author serves as publisher and retailer.

- Limited or no enforcement of usage rules or no usage rules

- Copyright protection is limited to copyrights afforded to all books.

   Here are examples of personal publishing include:

- The author writes an article or book that they want to make freely available to anyone who wants to read the book. The author may distribute the book via newsgroups or they may post it on the World Wide Web.

- The author creates a website and sells the electronic book using business commerce tools, such as a shopping cart, to handle credit card or electronic payment transactions. Users buy the book and download the book and there is neither tracking nor rights management involved. In this scenario, the author could as easily fulfill the user's request with an electronic book on a CD ROM or printed copy.

For personal publishing, the author does not have to consider tracking royalty payments or monitoring usage rights. Typically, the author's key concern is that their electronic book cannot be tampered with to create a forgery or, worse yet, to be rewritten. However, what the author does need to consider is that they will have to create the electronic book themselves or hire a service provider to create the book for them. Fortunately for authors, applications like Adobe Acrobat and Microsoft Reader enable authors to create an electronic book that protects the author's book from being modified. See Appendix C: Creating eBooks with Microsoft Word and Appendix D: Creating eBooks with Adobe Acrobat for information.

Subsidy or Vanity Publishing

Subsidy publishing or "vanity publishing" (though the term vanity publishing no longer fits, given that traditional publishers have funded companies to sell eBooks and pBooks from the World Wide Web) has created imprints focused on providing an outlet to first-time authors and niche books. Furthermore, companies have emerged that offer the following services to help authors publish directly to their readers.

- Conversion services to take content from many word processing programs and convert it into leading formats including Adobe Acrobat, Microsoft Reader, Gemstar, OEBF, Peanut Press, MobiPocket, XML, and other formats. If an author has content, a company will convert the content into a format that can be read by any of the leading electronic book hardware readers and software application readers.

- Conversion services to convert content if the author does not have the source files in an electronic format. Companies will scan hard copy into an electronic format and then convert the electronic format into an appropriate eBook format.

- DRM services to provide protection to the content. There are companies that provide not only DRM solutions but also host eBooks in a secure environment. Thus if an author wants to protect their content, they can find a service provider who will provide the service they need.

- Hosting services for eBook content and eCommerce tasks. Companies will provide space on a web server to make an eBook available and they will handle all eCommerce tasks such as credit card purchases and technical support.

- Print on demand (books on demand) services for authors who want to sell both an eBook and a pBook or just a pBook. These services include creating the digital files (typically PDF, TIFF, or PostScript) necessary for use on a digital printer and contracting a printer to print the pBook. In addition, these companies will fulfill distribution of the pBook to the user.

- Promotional services for authors are available for hire. One important point, which has always been true for self or vanity publishing, is that authors need to reach their audience to make them aware that the book is available. Companies not only offer the means to publish but also the means to market the book.

A key point about the companies who offer the above services is that these companies, unlike many "dot.coms", have business models that were proven in the past, subsidy and vanity publishers, and are working today. Simply put, these companies are usually profitable and exist on revenue, not venture capital. Below are a few examples of companies, both large and small, which are providing services to authors.

Barnes and Noble

Barnes and Noble, through its Digital Content Division, occupies an interesting place in ePublishing:, part publisher, part retailer, and part service provider. Here is a description of Barnes and Noble's ePublishing services:

- Conversion (scanning) of paper content into electronic content.

- Conversion of digital files in many common file formats to many electronic file formats that support both eBooks and print on demand (books on demand).

- Distribution services to enable authors to place their content with many eBook and print on demand (books on demand) companies.

1st Books

1st Books is a subsidy ePublishing company that specializes in helping authors to publish their books in both eBook and pBook format. Some of the services offered to authors by 1st Books are:

- Print on demand (through leading vendors) to enable authors to publish hard copy and paperback versions economically. Printed books can be shipped within two to three days from when the order is placed at a bookstore or online.

- The scanning of hard copy to create electronic books and electronic files for print on demand.

- The creation of eBooks from author's content for sale and distribution from the 1st Books website.

- The marketing of the author's book including press releases, Internet promotion, and advice on how authors can promote their books.

Some interesting points from the 1st Books business model is that authors pay for services such as preparing (which includes obtaining an ISBN for the book) paperback and hard cover (hard cover costs more) and for marketing services which are tiered in price based on the number of marketing services performed, including arranging for book signings. In essence, 1st Books duplicates, for a fee, the services provided by traditional publishers.

Another interesting fact is how royalties are set (as stated in 1st Books promotional materials, published in 2000):

- For eBooks: 100% of the first $300 of sales and 40 percent of the eBook price thereafter.

- For pBooks: 30% of the wholesale price.

Quality and ePublishing: Oxymoron?

One concern with the author-server-user model of publishing (and what has always been a concern with personal and subsidy publishing) is will an explosion of content lead to a complete cheapening of all books, whether eBooks or pBooks. Simply put, who will filter the content that reaches the reading public? Consider how content is filtered today in the traditional publishing model:

1. The author writes a book or writes an outline for a book and then needs to gain access to a publisher. The author either needs a literary agent or contacts the publisher directly. Depending upon the situation, there are two hurdles to clear: obtain a literary agent and obtain a contract with a publisher.

2. The author writes the book and the publisher performs an edit on the book. The author makes changes based on the publisher's edit. This represents the final hurdle for the author.

The gist of this is that the publisher is providing the author with a brand name to publish their book and thus both the author's and the publisher's reputations are bound together; each has an obligation to provide the best content they can. However, with personal or subsidy publishing, who provides the filtering other than the author? Will this lead to a depreciation of content? Alternatively, are the skills of the authors sufficient to provide appreciable content?

Quality Reviews

At a presentation I made before a group of authors, I stated that the textbook market was probably one of the best markets for eBooks (see *Chapter 9: Oligarchy of New Media* for more information on this topic) and one writer, who had published several textbooks for a well-known publisher, stated that this would have a negative impact on textbooks because textbook publishers performed many important tasks, including the very important task of verifying facts in the textbooks. The author also stated that fact checking was a key reason why textbooks were not updated frequently and this contradicts a selling point of electronic textbooks; frequent updates. Is it possible to update textbooks more frequently while making sure the facts are correct?

Having written a few technical manuals in my career, I remember how the review cycles permitted as many as three reviews but, as product cycles shortened, review cycles shortened to perhaps one review. The temptation of ePublishing is to speed up the publishing cycle at potentially, the expense of reviewing the content. For genres like textbooks, this could lead to a deprecation of the genre.

Along these lines, at the NIST 2000 conference, *eBook: Changing the Fundamentals of Reading*, there was a discussion by a panel, which included an author, literary agent, and three publishers, about how users would find quality eBooks on the World Wide Web. Some suggested that online reviews of eBooks would suffice; others suggested that the market place would filter quality by publishing only successful eBooks.

Eventually though, establishing a brand name as an author, whether as an expert in some technology, some period of history, or whatever, successful authors will emerge and users will go to the companies on the World Wide Web who offer access to these successful authors. It is very likely that these companies will represent a majority of the traditional publishers and a few of the new ePublishing companies.

Another source of quality control may be your local librarians as described in *Chapter 9: Oligarchy of New Media, World Library of the Future*.

Chapter 8: A View from the Gallery

"eBooks are about 50% technology; 50% culture". Thierry Brethes, MobiPocket, 2001

What the Experts Say

After prattling along for many pages, it seems appropriate to hear what experts in the field of electronic books have to say about the future of electronic books and ePublishing. The experts were selected based on their involvement and experience in the industry. Key among the selection were these factors: people who had opinions to express that represented not the talking head opinions you hear or see on television or read in magazines but people who have perspective as well as vision and perhaps equally important, a sense of humor.

Each expert was asked a set of three questions: the first and second questions were the same for each person so you can compare answers and the third question was written specifically for that person.

Hubris or Passion?

Having worked for 20 years at IBM in product development, I can remember the excitement (and pride) when a product was shipped and customers bought it. Nevertheless, the excitement was always tempered because as soon as the product was shipped, it was time to begin work on the next product.

In the nascent electronic book industry, the enthusiasm you encounter is more than an enthusiasm for potential profits; it is the enthusiasm of people who love books and publishing. There is a common bond amongst the industry practitioners (yes, even the marketing people) that is a bond of people who are trying to change the way we read, a task that almost has the aura of a crusade. In the comments below, besides insight and perspective, the enthusiasm for ebooks and ePublishing is clear. That enthusiasm is an important element in the potential success of the eBook and ePublishing industry.

Question One: It's Been Tried Before, Why Now?

The electronic book is not a new idea and the past is littered with failed attempts including efforts from hardware vendors like Sony who, in 1990, marketed the Bookman/Dataman, and publishers like World Library, who in 1990 published the Electronic Classical Library, and in 1994 published, Will and Ariel Durant's, The Story of Civilization. Yet, in both instances, each company met with some initial success but ultimately failed. Why should the concept of electronic books and electronic book readers succeed now?

Daniel Munyan, Everybook

There is only one reason why electronic books will succeed this time or fail as in earlier attempts. Content. Content is king. Not a hundred titles, or a thousand, or ten thousand. From my experience, there must be at least 50,000 titles available 12 months from now, and not just any 50,000 titles. It must include all college textbooks used on campuses today. It must include all of the bestseller lists. It must include all newspapers, the majority of magazines, and all K-12 textbooks. Anything less than all of the documents in common use today will lead to a failure of the eBook industry.

Secondly, there must be a standard for all electronic documents that will allow any of those 50,000 titles to be read on a PC, Mac, laptop, electronic reader, or PDA. The security for authors must require a password to open a title or to transfer it (NOT COPY) to another device. Consumers must be able to transfer (preferably by wireless mode) any of the titles they own from one device to another.

Publishers, authors, and distributors will have to be willing to split a much smaller profit pie. They will have to rely on the ability of the Net to sell their publications worldwide at much larger, tax-free volumes. Publication costs will have to drop 50% across the board. Publishers will have to find ways to market books less expensively through targeted advertising on the Net.

Wayne Forte, IBM

Consumers are familiar with and accept the Internet as a source of not only information but also now consumables. It is now commonplace for the consumer to shop for the consumable goods such as airline tickets, gasoline and even food. This shift in the paradigm sets the stage for a successful eBook platform.

Mike Riley, RR Donnelley & Sons Company

I am not entirely certain that eBooks will succeed *now*, but they will ultimately succeed in the future. The purpose-built eBook devices of today are the Bomar(tm) calculators of the eBook world. The current generation of devices projects a glimpse of what the future has in store.

Compared to past efforts, the most noticeable advantage that today's eBook devices have over early attempts, like the Sony Bookman/Dataman, is the screen display size and resolution. Still, these two simple metrics need to be substantially improved (which they will be) before the mass consumer market wholly embraces the technology. Today, the current generation of devices will be adopted by ardent book readers and rabid technologists. But like the history of personal computers, these specialized markets will evangelize and develop better solutions to a point in time when e-reading will supersede analog reading for the masses.

Warren Adler, Author

Why now? The technology moves forward relentlessly, always very much ahead of the market. As, increasingly, people, especially the young and yet unborn, acquire the skills of the computer; their world becomes "cyberspaced". They get used to reading text on screens. Paper books become less convenient and more expensive; delivery of content becomes easier.

Reading of "books" on a screen is inevitable in the future. As for the marketing aspect, the business model of homogenized mass communications in every aspect of our lives becomes more fractionalized. The bestseller as we now know it will yield to smaller bestsellers, more diverse, less mass. The coming of the eBook is no longer a question mark. It will come. It is coming. The history of new things is studded with failures as the concepts lurch forward, but the forward movement cannot be stopped.

Will Manis, Microsoft

Success is a subjective thing, but what I think we will see is the introduction of technologies and standards that will evolve into a true consumer experience. We have proven that we can create devices that allow immersive reading on screen, a huge step forward, we have created standards that publishers are willing to embrace to store their assets; we have created security systems that protect the intellectual property of authors and publishers and we have proved that there is a market place for eBooks.

The creation of a consumer market will not happen overnight, we are still too early for true consumer devices. A true consumer device is at a price point that is effectively an impulse, or at the least, not an overly considered purchase, probably in the $150 range. It will be a while before we have a high-quality reading device at that price point.

Why now or at least why are we on the way? Everything is coming together that will foster a healthy industry of delivery of electronic content to devices. The benefits of reading on screen will outweigh the benefits of reading on paper, until recently that has not been the case. Our kids are walking to school with backpacks that weigh 30% of their body weight, busy people want personalized content delivered wherever they may be, the traveling public does not want to tote 6 novels, 4 maps, 8 guide books and a separate GPS system to Paris for their summer vacation. This is a confluence of communications, screen technology, processing power and consumer need.

Thierry Brethes, MobiPocket

The concept of the eBook will succeed now due to the combination of:

1. The generalization of wired/wireless Internet access to everyone at a low cost. The Internet will be used for both buying eBooks and downloading content. This was not the case 10 years ago, where the distribution channel to reach millions of people did not exist.

2. The generalization of the use of multi-function devices: PCs (300 million connected to the Internet) and PDAs (20 million by the end of 2000, 40 million in 2001) that enable everybody to buy eBooks without buying dedicated specific hardware. This is why I do not believe in dedicated eBook hardware devices like Rocket eBook.

3. The obvious advantage in terms of cost to the end user: eBooks could be sold at 50% of the price of paper book, while keeping the same profit for authors, publishers and retailers.

4. The massive digitalization process to open-eBook publications under way by all major publishers worldwide.

Ken Hoffman, Rochester Institute of Technology

In general, I believe that electronic book formats will supplement, but not replace, the paper book over the next couple of decades. There is now, and most likely will continue to be, a comfort level with the permanence, portability, and tangibility about the paper book. The novel, the display or "coffee table" book, the anthology of poetry or essays, and even the textbook all benefit from these characteristics.

There is something very appealing about being able to take a book anywhere. Which would you rather do: spill coffee on a paper book or on an eBook electronic device? Which would you rather drop? Which would you rather risk leaving on a plane, bus, or subway? While paper is certainly not permanent, it is considerably more so than the myriad of changing file formats which continually are introduced, evolve, and pass on to the digital beyond. Will the device of today be able to open an eBook file in ten years? Will the eBook device of 2011 be able to open the eBook file of today? I can guarantee that I will still be able to read one of my favorite books from my father's library in 2011 when that book is almost 150 years old.

However, books in electronic format are ideal for a wide variety of books in which content is not meant to be read in a linear way and which will benefit from having interactive, searchable, and media capabilities. Digital publishing workflows will easily accommodate the parallel publishing of both printed books and eBooks. Digital book production will be necessary and driven by an increase in the book-on-demand market.

Roger Fidler, Kent State University

Until recently, the display technology and text rendering software used in portable reading devices were unable to provide a comfortable reading experience and were not ready for the general consumer market – the resolution and contrast were too low for reading in diverse lighting conditions; the screens were too small; the typography and presentation formats were too limited; battery life was too short; the price was too high; and the available eBook titles was too limited.

There were some success stories, however. Franklin, for example, produced a number of successful dedicated handheld reading devices in the early 1990s that contained reference materials, such as dictionaries, encyclopedias, and specialized desk references.

Andrew Dillon, Indiana University

There is a certain inevitability to the digital transformation of information that demands our development of more usable eBooks. I would not view the early failures as anything more than the normal evolutionary process of product development that usually involves several iterations of a new design before a product succeeds. Just think of the first airplanes or cars and you will see how new products require some inevitable failures before succeeding.

Why should the eBook be any different? Well, I suppose people think that their design is so much simpler but I would counter that any technology that is aimed at a human user can rarely be seen as too simple to require testing. I would, of course, also point out that the earliest eBook designs were rather pointless from a user's point of view, offering little of the value of computers in a physical form that was far less suited than paper to the uses people made of such texts. As we learn to combine the power of computers with the quality of paper that is so natural to us, I think future products will be better. But let me say this: I do not believe we will really see eBooks replacing paper. Rather we shall see graceful co-existence, with eBooks being used to generate paper versions.

Victor McCrary, National Institute of Standards

Think about the environment of the late 80s: personal computers, PCs, were just making there way into the business environment, but only a small percentage of consumers purchased for home use. The Web did not exist, and most home and office PC's been used as stand-alone machines. Wireless telephony was limited to the privileged, and PDA's were still on the drawing boards.

Looking back at that environment, consumers had no experience with portable, mobile devices; behavior at that time was limited to wire line phones, and stand-alone PCs. Those earlier "e-book-like" devices failed because users had no experiential base to tie these devices into the business environment (remember the PC in the business environment was a bridge in terms of usability from the VT-100-like "dumb" terminals connected to company mainframes).

Now fast-forward to 2001: over 47% of the U.S. is on-line, PDA's and cell phones are cultural icons, and the ability to obtain information "when I want it and where I want it" is paramount and part of today's social fabric. Digital convergence is bringing computing and consumer electronics together to offer digital content in many ways. With so much information to absorb, today's scarce resource is time and convenience. Electronic books in the form of digitized content, will succeed because they save time because content can be accessed wherever there is a connection to the Internet. E-Books are convenient because they offer portability by virtue of the storage of megabytes of digital content; i.e., many books! Let's face it, shelf space a premium for all of us at home or in the office.

Future e-book readers will also incorporate functions of today's PDAs- contact manager, e-mail, as well as be your telephone. The "Super-PDA" will allow a richer reading experience (color screens, clearer fonts, reduced surface glare, improved contrast ratio) and be multi-functional. Consumers are currently adverse towards carrying more devices on their belts or in their purses. The correct mix of features will evolve.

Question Two: Evolution or Revolution?

The premise of this book is that the electronic book represents an evolution from the paper book to electronic format and, initially, electronic books should use the best features of the paper book, such as the table of contents and indexes, to reduce the learning curve and provide a transition for users from the paper book to the electronic book. Many researchers disagree with this premise and suggest that this approach fails to take advantage of technology and instead authors should focus on designing new ways to package information and discard book features. Five years from now, what will an electronic book look like?

Daniel Munyan, Everybook

It depends what you mean by an electronic book. If you mean the device, I expect there to be a range of devices. One will be a PDA/cell phone combination, small, light, and cheap, with a three or four inch square, high resolution, color screen. Another will be a PC laptop device that is about 8.5"x11", very light, with a keyboard, and a high-resolution, color, plastic screen. The third will be a two-screen laptop equivalent with fully abutting

LCD/touchscreens that double as a drawing pad, multimedia player, and at a pinch, a laptop with a virtual keyboard. I expect that as technology becomes smaller, lighter, cheaper, and more common, reading systems will become more organic in nature. As glass gives way to plastic in screens, as batteries become polymer-based, and as magnesium becomes more common in casing, devices will become much lighter and far less prone to damage by heat and impact. I expect the return of the leather book cover and other affectations surrounding very advanced technology.

If by electronic book you mean the content, I expect most publications to appear exactly as they do today. Newspapers will change from broadsheet to tabloid format, but the other documents will remain similar to today's two-page design. Nothing I have seen or read about hyperlinks in training documents changes my mind about how people read and learn. I expect that a person will be reading an electronic book five years from now, in a two-page layout, with text, figures, tables and illustrations. I expect however, that the tables and illustrations will come to life with a touch, linking to websites and multimedia files. But the technological enhancements will take place within the ordered layout of a page within a chapter, within a book, within a collection, within a library of sorts.

Many technologists seem to miss the point that our hands, eyes, and brains have not changed, even though our minds and perceptions have evolved. From the beginning of writing until now, the format of the book has remained essentially the same in proportion, representation of information, contrast requirements, and layout. Carpal Tunnel Syndrome, increased eyestrain, and other modern maladies remind us that we are cavemen in khakis and Docsiders. We are ill equipped to work for long with keyboards and mice, backlights and batteries. We have built special furniture for our technology, cloistered it in climate-controlled rooms, fed it enormous amounts of electricity, and learned new languages in order to interact with it. This just has to stop. The cost and inefficiencies, the learning curve and class distinctions it fosters, all are nasty by-products of the early years of the computer revolution. I expect the nanotechnological age to return us to tools with a simple, classic appearance, which mold to us and interact with us on the human level, not the machine level. I believe that books represent the chasm that technology cannot cross without "re-humanizing".

Wayne Forte, IBM

I believe that the eBook will continue to look like its ancestors, but slowly transition into a truly emmersive multimedia experience. The click of a mouse will allow the reader to view and hear JFK's inauguration speech, or even to be taken to other related content sites quickly and with ease.

Mike Riley, RR Donnelley & Company

Five years are multiple product lifetimes in the computing world, and hence my belief is that the e-reading landscape will be unlike anything we can imagine today. With the fascinating improvements promised over the next five years in display, storage, power and communication (including broadband and wireless) technologies, many infrastructure limitations that stymie electronic publishers of content today will be eliminated.

The one problematic area that I believe will persist is the question of cross-platform, industry-standardized Digital Rights Management. There is simply no easy solution I can foresee on the horizon for this requirement to be met uniformly within the next five years.

Still, it IS easy to predict that eReading devices will get smarter and more interactive over such a timeframe. They will also become less expensive and more durable. It is even quite possible that, with faster CPU's, more memory and storage capacity of these devices will develop a kind of personality and rapport for their owners, using such things as AI routines to know how fast their owners read an average page (based on the click through rate, for example) and tailor that reading pace depending on the type of content (highly technical content may progress at a slower rate than a detective novel, for example).

Other aspects such as gender preference, highly targeted content interest typing via DOI (Digital Object Identifier)-style recall, and wireless on-demand viewing could be features in 5+

year eReading devices. Biometric sensors could even be employed in the device, such as a small camera just above the display that would scan for basic facial expressions of joy, sorrow, concern, confusion and the book's content could react accordingly. An additional biometric control could be placed on the power switch which, when depressed, would only power the device and/or display a particular document when the person was authorized to do so (this makes it a lot easier than remembering passwords or dealing with complex digital signing processes).

Warren Adler, Author

Critical mass will make a revolution out of evolution. As more and more people tune into the eBook market, it will suddenly seem like an evolution. Indeed, the amount of money being poured into every facet of this "revolution" is astonishing. We will soon enter the most important phase, simple inexpensive portable ergonomics with easy access to content. Books as we now know them will be very expensive antiques. Schoolchildren will carry their entire textbook education in their pockets. The major publishers know this and are kicking themselves for their lack of vision.

Will Manis, Microsoft

It is an evolution and not a revolution. Look at any new media. Photography – the early photographers mimicked painters, until they figured out that they could do things much differently than painters. The same for film early cinematographers pointed their film cameras at the stage, eventually D.W. Griffith discovered that they could pan, do close ups, do long shots and various other cinema graphic tricks, away from the traditional theatrical stage and create an entirely new medium. The same will happen for eBooks: we will mimic the printed book until this medium's D.W. Griffith or Ernie Kovacs comes along and turns it on its head. As technology providers, we can only aspire to provide these creative individuals with tools for them to create their magic.

Thierry Brethes, MobiPocket

eBook is an evolution, not a revolution. The first step, which will take about 5-10 years, will be to have the existing paperback/CD ROM content available for eBooks. This will mean no major modification of the content but a "porting".

In a second step, when devices and technologies become more mature and stable, authors will naturally change the way they write, or at least adapt it to the new reading devices. You could ask the same question about PCs and keyboards: did the introduction of the keyboard and the replacement of pens for writing content change the way people write documents/books? Not very much.

Ken Hoffman, Rochester Institute of Technology

Highly interactive, reader friendly, searchable, usable, and entertaining books; packed with audio and video media; customized content, including user-specific images and text (great for customized kid's eBooks) file compression formats will make eBooks with compact file size, yet high quality for both static and dynamic content; perhaps fewer device-dependent eBooks in a more open file-exchange world; likewise, eBook devices will be able to open multiple file formats; security for protecting eBook files from unauthorized copying and distribution will continue to be an issue.

Roger Fidler, Kent State University

I agree with your premise that the electronic book represents an evolution rather than a revolution in publishing. I do not believe we should throw away 500 years of publishing experience and start over with no links to the past.

History confirms that when new media are introduced – mechanical printing, film, radio, television, World Wide Web – they typically blend the formats and functions of established media with the value-adding features provided by new technologies.

I firmly believe that for a new medium to be successful in the general consumer market, it must provide users with a bridge of familiarity. In the case of ePublishing, content should be page-based and presented in predominantly portrait-orientation. All essential visual clues, such as chapter headings, page numbers, subheads, etc., should be retained. I also do not believe any of the essential affordances of traditional print media should be sacrificed, such as the ability to highlight and markup text, bookmark pages, make copies of pages, etc., nor do I believe that the features provided by newer technology should add complexity for the user. People should not be required to read a manual before they can read an eBook or ePeriodical.

Andrew Dillon, Indiana University

The answer is neither all or nothing. We do know, or at least we should know by now, that parroting the analog form of anything into a digital version is a poor way of attempting to make progress. So much of what makes the analog device successful is lost in the electronic world so we do need to think more broadly and more innovatively if we seek to create new digital tools.

On the other hand, that is not a recommendation to dump everything we know and start designing eBooks as if there were no parallels with the paper world to draw upon. When designers talk of mimicking access mechanisms, like the tables of contents etc., they should be less concerned with the physical matching of the worlds than with the cognitive structures such mechanisms afford users. Information is structured, by the author, the book layout designer, and by the reader upon consumption. Depending on context, we want those structures to match and good design enables this.

My dream for eBooks is that they enable even greater capabilities to restructure information according to contextual variables such as preference, ability, knowledge and so forth. Add to this more seamless integration with related information sources and one can see a new form of information space made possible by technology. But any design, no matter how radical, runs smack into perceptual, cognitive, physiological and social processes of users and use. The parameters set by these processes are far less flexible in many ways than the technology and we would be well served by studying them more rather than worrying too much about what features of the paper world we should emulate. That is a radical recommendation for design but I see no other way forward in the long term. Evolution through revolution perhaps, but evolution no less.

Victor McCrary, National Institute of Standards

R2. New forms of content presentation and dissemination are always encouraged. However, the first rule of product design is to make sure the new product (or service) provides an easy bridge from the consumer's previous experience.

Five years from now, people will still be reading left to right, expecting column formats for periodicals, and highlights in specialized media like textbooks and manuals. As more digital content becomes available, there will be an abundance of opportunities for content creators and software developers to display (no pun intended!) their talents. E-Books will spawn the era of "recombinant media" where e-book files will contain a mix of text, images, video and music --- a feat not accomplishable when these forms of content are analog (hence for years separate businesses in publishing, printing, television, cinema, and recording).   Ultimately, digital convergence allows a broader offering to the consumer. For example, imagine you could purchase the $9.95 e-book version of L. Frank Baum's The Wizard of OZ, which is just plain text and a few black-n-white drawings. Or you could purchase the $24.99 e-book version offering color pictures, a side biography of L. Frank Baum, video clips of the 1939 Warner Studios cinema version of *The Wizard of Oz*, video clips from the 1978 Universal modern version (*The Wiz*), and finally an audio track of Judy Garland singing *Somewhere Over the Rainbow*!!! What's intriguing about this example is that consumers have the experience of choosing different packaging of the same content -- like the gold, collector's series of videotapes, which contain additional film clips.

Question Three: A Question for Each Expert

Note: each expert was asked a unique question based on their expertise and their experience within the industry. Below are the questions and the expert's answers.

Daniel Munyan, Everybook

You were a pioneer in the electronic book industry well before the current product offerings and your focus for the Everybook Journal had been the display of two pages, 8.5 by 11 inches, which gave users the complete look and feel of a "real book". Moreover, in your new product, DocAble, you continue to use paper metaphors for ease of use. Is it important for electronic books to use metaphors based on paper books? If so, why?

I believe that documents based on paper metaphors of layout, font, and pagination require paper metaphor management systems. DocAble replaces the Drive/Directory/File database system designed for unformatted (in the document sense) data files and application programs with the paper metaphors of bookshelves, three-ring binders, and vertical tabs crafted for documents. Our visual organization system, which we call the Worktable, allows users the ability to create, view, and organize collections of documents in ways that Windows Explorer cannot do. Whether a document is located on a hard drive, CD ROM, intranet, web, or LAN should be irrelevant to a user that wants to organize a document collection for his or her own purposes. The end-user's document organization should have no effect on the enterprise document storage, security, and distribution system as well. Our FileScout, Autoindexing, Cross-collection search engine, and Synchronization features automate and integrate document management and control functions that exist in other programs as separate, unrelated features that must be studiously learned to be used.

We allow users to work with multiple documents simultaneously without moving them into and out of the background. We integrate reading and writing, research and citation, annotation and workflow in the same way that paper-based systems integrate them.

Wayne Forte, IBM

IBM has had success in providing Digital Rights Management technology to the music industry. Are the issues and technology in the music industry the same as in the book publishing industry?

The fundamental issues of piracy protection and privacy of the consumer are the same, and the technology to protect the content is similar. There are inherent differences between music and eBook file types that must be prepared and treated differently. The real difference between music and eBooks is in the eMerchandising and eSelling of the content. Publishers and content owners of eBooks need complex usage rules and business models to accommodate the legacy methods of selling and to foster new revenue streams for the content that is the real payback.

Mike Riley, RR Donnelley & Company

RR Donnelley & Company was one of the founding members of the Open Electronic Book Forum and has successfully embraced electronic workflows in printing. What is the future of printers in the ePublishing world? Is it technologies like print on demand, electronic book publishing, or traditional offset printing?

eBooks and POD will have a difficult time completely usurping the economics of high-volume ink on paper. Instead, I believe these two forms of content communication (digital versus analog) will coexist and present an author or publisher with economic choices for the type of market they wish to deliver their product to. For publishers, believing eBooks are simply electronic versions of identical content available in print, and therefore not adding any additional, incremental value by leveraging the potential of this technology, is a mistake and a gross misuse of the platform. For instance, just as DVD's support a plethora of enhancements (bonus materials, making of' featurettes, director commentary, slick index presentations, etc.) that extend the value beyond VHS tapes for movies, so too must publishers adopt a strategy that leverages the advanced technological content features that these devices can support. It is RR Donnelley's commitment to insure that we provide trusted services to our publishing customers that exceed these expectations.

Warren Adler, Author

You are an established and bestselling author who has created their own virtual bookstore to sell your "roster" of books and thus you have become both an author and a publisher. You describe this as a "gift of empowerment" for authors. Can you explain this a little further?

For the author this means megawatt empowerment. He or she is no longer at the mercy of the publisher in terms of distribution and marketing. The editing functions will be taken over by editing boutiques and authors will be devising their own methods of marketing with the invaluable help of the online sellers who are moving. At this juncture it is the author, like myself, with a large backlist, who is the principal beneficiary. The big issue for the author will be marketing and this will require a financial investment in his authorial brand.

Both the new and old media will be needed to create awareness and bring readers into the fold. Authors will now be able to identify their readers, harvest them, communicate with them, and establish a family of readership. A drawback for the author will be the vast database of content. It will be up to the author to blast himself out of the database and increase his awareness if this is to succeed for him.

Will Manis, Microsoft

Microsoft successfully launched the Microsoft Reader which has provided an excellent book reading experience on devices ranging from desktops to Pocket PCs. Bill Gates, in his book, The Road Ahead, described how homes will include computers that enable a homeowner to ask that their favorite book be displayed from room to room so they can read it at home as they move about or sit in their favorite room. How far are we from integrating the electronic book reading experience into the home?

Reading is a private experience; I do not believe we will read on a screen across the room. That being said, we are well on the way to providing access to one's library "anywhere, anytime", and that library will be much more than just a collection of documents: it will provide searching, sorting, annotating, sharing and many more features, all part of an "active reading" experience.

Thierry Brethes, MobiPocket

Your company has pioneered publishing and reading tools for PDA devices and, importantly, you are a European company with a global perspective. Do you believe that electronic books will be available in many languages or will the language of electronic books be primarily English, as is currently the case with the majority of content available on the Internet? From your website, it would appear that content is growing in other languages, is this a correct impression?

Of course, the United States always takes the lead for any technological innovation in the Internet, but as the eBook is about 50% technology and 50% culture, I expect a lot of European publishers/retailers to produce and sell a huge amount of eBooks in French, German, and so on. Some major European publishers, like Vivendi Universal Publishing (formerly Havas) have made important investments to produce all their content into open-eBook format.

Ken Hoffman, Rochester Institute of Technology

You are an expert in publishing workflows and have been watching trends, such as digital print on demand and the impact of digital printing on publishing. Do you think that shorter print runs are the norm in traditional book publishing?

I do not have specific current data but, yes, this market segment has also been impacted by the economics of print. The costs associated with getting to press have decreased with digital prepress workflows. Pressroom and bindery productivity have also been improved. Therefore, the cost per unit has declined enough to make smaller book print run lengths profitable without an excessive increase in book costs. Publishers do not need to plan long run lengths in order to maintain cost-competitive book prices; risk for overrun is lessened. Books that historically have had short run lengths, such as college textbooks, may still be printed with short run lengths but benefit from workflow improvements.

Where does scrap occur in traditional printing: first or later editions?

Again, I do not have specific data, but my understanding is that book publishing is still faced with the possibility that book sales will not match closely with production totals. Initial edition run lengths can be incorrectly estimated today as easily as in the past. It is also true for later edition run lengths. The experience of the publisher with specific authors, topics, styles, etc. is highly valued when determining production run lengths. Some books sell out first editions quickly and easily; others have a large percentage of unsold units. With the increasing capability for book-on-demand digital printing, I expect publishers to be conservative in their offset print run lengths. Of course, the out-of-print concept will disappear.

Roger Fidler, Kent State University

How important are standards? Kent State, through the Future of Print Media Journal, has been a valuable source of information on the electronic book industry and one of the studies published in the Future of Print Media Journal (1998) indicated that students seemed willing to accept and, perhaps as importantly, pay for electronic books as long as they believed that electronic books would be able to be viewed on any electronic book reader, much as in the way an audio compact disc can be played on any player. Do you feel the industry has made progress on this issue? In essence, is there enough cooperation in the industry?

The ePublishing standard are essential. All ePublications intended for general audiences should be readable on all consumer eReader devices. The nascent eBook industry is making progress on eBook standards, but I believe it will take several more years before eContent and eReading devices are truly interoperable.

The main problems today are proprietary Digital Rights Management systems and closed publishing systems that require consumers to buy dedicated eBook reading devices that can only access and/or buy ePublications from the vendor's site. At this stage, each vendor is trying to control the market and to force everyone else to adopt its standard.

Until eBooks and eBook reading devices incorporate interoperable standards, I believe the majority of consumers will be hesitant to purchase eBook reading devices and ePublications.

Andrew Dillon, Indiana University

In 1994, you published Designing Usable Electronic Text, and in your book, you stated that the acceptance of electronic books could be accelerated by good design or hampered by weak design. Now, six plus years later, do you feel the acceptance of electronic books is being accelerated or hampered by the design of the electronic book content?

I am gratified in some senses that what has come to pass, namely the web and PDAs, only makes that point more obvious now than it might have been in the early 1990s. Like most things in life, there are two aspects to this issue which reflect competing forces. The web has shown how hungry the world is for access to digital documents and there is no going back. People are empowered by the range of material that is accessible online and the acceptance level for eText is high. Yet, most people, when faced with large masses of text online that they need to read will resort to printing it out on paper. This, coupled with the standing argument that you cannot take an eBook to bed with you, is used to argue that eBooks have no real future.

For me, the print issue is no big deal. I suspect dual-form texts will be the norm - the graceful co-existence issue I mentioned earlier will be standard. So, in that case, the future is not a matter of digital OR paper, but digital and paper, each exploited as it best suits the context of use.

The physical issue, the dislike many of us have to the tactile and perceptual qualities of eBook devices is also a temporary phenomenon I believe. The current technological implementations of eBooks are just that, current implementations. Future technologies that allow us to project screens onto our walls, or even into the visual space in front of us, might render physicality a non-issue. Imagine a book on demand that appeared where you were, sized in space and movable according to your preferences but really only being a projection, not a handheld reader. Now that would change a few minds.

And of course let us never forget the context issue - some eBooks are so much more useful and usable than paper equivalents in some tasks. Imagine trying to use only paper documents to look up telephone numbers or to locate specific quotes that you know are "somewhere" in the text. Again, the leveraging of computer power in appropriate contexts makes the future of eBooks inevitable. My concern is that we use good design as a means of exploiting this power sooner rather than later – and, in my view, current designers are not doing this nearly as well as they should. The issues are only partly technical. A huge part of the solution lies in a better understanding of users, which I believe is where I ended up in 1994 and will probably still end up when I retire :).

Victor McCrary, National Institute of Standards

NIST enabled the nascent electronic book industry to get off the ground by helping to form the OEBF and sponsoring three conferences that brought together industry with consumers; what is next for NIST and the ebook industry?

NIST is the most appropriate agency as part of the U.S. Department of Commerce to help catalyze new industries by facilitating standards and interoperability. We are glad that the industry solicited and welcomes our leadership in facilitating version 1.0 of the Open Electronic Book (OEB) Publication Structure Standard and our efforts in forming the Open eBook Forum (OEBF). Many publishers port digital content via OEB, and the OEBF is the definitive standards and trade organization for e-books.

We view e-books as a small piece in the larger pie of digital publishing. Publishing, in the traditional sense, no longer evokes images of cold type and inked presses --- it's more about composition on computers, print-on-demand, digital image manipulation, and trust in material quality. That is why a Doubleday e-book will still be worth more than an Acme e-book. More added value, more willingness to pay! Finally "publishing" also includes placing content on other dissemination platforms; e.g. DVD. Again the phenomenon of digital convergence brings together storage technology and publishing.

For NIST, we see ourselves bringing the industry together to discuss and dissect the entire digital publishing value chain to identify both technical and business challenges that face the industry. These issues include trust management (i.e. digital rights management, assurance of quality), preservation of digital content, hardware interoperability, software conformance, accessibility of digital content, and content quality (e.g. color fidelity on different display platforms). The NIST Measurement and Standards Laboratories are extremely skilled at tackling these issues. We also bring to the table our role as being neutral: we work through our collaborations with the U.S. industry in creating wealth and improving the quality of American life.

For instance, we developed a prototype, low-cost, rotating wheel Braille reader that can read an OEB file, thus making e-books accessible to the visually impaired. As we proceed towards the future digital world, we all will be empowered to express ourselves as artists, because software and hardware will converge to make it easy for us to capture, manipulate, edit, and combine all forms of digital content to our own creative touch. My vision is that NIST will play a key role unleashing the power and inspiration we all will gain from digital convergence. I'm really excited as the future unfolds!

Chapter 9: Oligarchy of New Media

"I have said that the medium is the message in the long run...Print simply wiped out the main modes of oral education...and the manuscript throughout the medieval period. And it ended that twenty-five-hundred-year pattern in a few decades. Today, the monarchy of print has ended and an oligarchy of new media has usurped most of the power of that five-hundred-year-old monarchy." Marshall McLuhan, 1959

Previous Medium Provides the New Medium

For better and more likely for worse, this section describes (or is it predicts) some future developments in electronic publishing and electronic books. McLuhan's oligarchy consisted of radio and television and now that oligarchy could be expanded to include the World Wide Web. Will electronic books represent a force that once again places books among the oligarchy?

Kenner (1984) described McLuhan's premise that new mediums arise from old mediums when he stated "Marshal McLuhan noticed long ago that the content of a medium is always a previous medium. He also remarked that we do not see a medium itself, save as a packaging for its content. That helps ease new media into acceptability. Genteel folk once learned to tolerate movies by thinking of them as packaged plays or packaged books...word processing is another incantation. Souls are safe in proximity to words".

So, what are the new mediums that will emerge from the old mediums? Specifically what will arise besides electronic books from the medium we call paper books?

Electronic Paper

Electronic paper may be the new medium that truly is preceded by an old medium, paper. Electronic paper is defined as a medium, typically plastic, that is embedded with beads, chips, or microcapsules and when electricity is passed through the beads, chips, or microcapsules, letters and pictures are formed.

Figure 14: Electronic Ink and Paper

Of course, referring to electronic paper as a new medium is somewhat inaccurate; the concept was conceived in the 1970s at Xerox PARC labs by Nick Sheridan (Klein, 2000). This was part of Xerox's concept of the paperless office which, like electronic paper, has not quite arrived yet.

Benefits of Electronic Paper

Benefits of electronic paper are:

- It provides the look and feel of paper, which includes the tactile feel of paper. The electronic paper could be handled like paper including folding for reading.

- It provides resolution as good as and more likely better than current computer displays.

- It enables content to be updated frequently as the paper is fully reusable.

- It updates content in "real-time" using wireless technology to provide, for example, real-time newspapers.

- It replaces content with new content (read one book and then change to another book).

- It provides portability as the electronic paper can be rolled up and carried like a newspaper or scroll (like in science fiction movies).

- It supplies its own power source, as very little power is required to charge the beads, chips, or microcapsules.

- It arranges the electronic paper into bound books, posters, or can be worn on you shirt to proclaim your favorite cause or sports team.

Design Goals of Electronic Paper

The design goals for electronic paper as cited by the *Economist* (2000), Kidner (2000), and Xerox (2000) for include the following:

- It must match the reading experience of paper because paper is read using reflected light and our eyes have adjusted or been trained to read paper with reflected light. Electronic paper should have an advantage over computer displays because of the use of reflected light.

- It must provide a form factor similar to paper that includes thickness, varying sizes, and flexibility.

- It must support input devices, such as a wand, that can provide input onto the paper.

- It must update content using wireless technology.

- It must maintain the text and pictures until the user chooses to replace or update it.

- It must not consume power once the text and pictures have been formed.

- The price must be far less than current displays and not too much more than paper. Though, it is important to note when comparing costs between paper and electronic paper, electronic paper is reusable.

Science Fiction or Fact?

There are some very well-known names involved in the development of electronic paper including: E Ink (spun out from Massachusetts Institute of Technology), Hearst, IBM, Lucent, Motorola, and Xerox (through its subsidiary, Gyricon), and 3M (which may manufacture electronic paper for Xerox). Electronic paper is already being used in department stores to display advertisements that can be updated often and it has also been used in some newspaper operations, most notably the *Arizona Republic*.

What is fascinating about electronic paper is the goal of developers to make a product that looks, feels, and functions like paper while providing functions that paper cannot provide, such as automatic updates. As Jim Iuliano, of E Ink stated "I live with computers, but I don't like to spend hours and hours reading on them...I don't think LCD [displays] goes away but I think paper and paper-like technology is better for immersive reading" (Rushlo, 2000).

Along those lines, Kenneth Bronfin from the Hearst Corporation, stated that electronic paper represented a medium that truly supports traditional reading, "This [electronic paper] is something people can curl up in bed with, whereas they won't curl up in bed with a device that looks like a computer and has glass and batteries. This is a device that will actually look and feel a lot like a book" (Ritter, 1998).

While there is often much hype associated with the nascent electronic book industry, the *Economist* (2000) summed up the potential of electronic paper: "Newspapers, books, posters, walls and even t-shirts will no longer be passive objects with fixed messages printed on them. They will become interactive, animated and even change by the hour." Couple this with a media that can be read like paper, acts like paper, but provides more function than paper, and we may see the perfect electronic book within ten years.

A more optimistic prediction is offered by Jim Iuliano of E Ink, who said: "There are no obstacles to electronic books [created with electronic paper] by 2003 or 2004. It's not ten or seven years out, I'd be stunned if it's even five years out" (Maney, 2000). Given the importance of providing users with a technology that takes advantage of the best attributes of the old technology (paper) and adds those attributes into the new technology (electronic paper), we can hope that Iuliano's prediction is proven true.

Textbooks: No More Backpacks

Probably the most profitable and valuable segment of the ePublishing industry is textbooks. Why, because this genre commands a high retail price, which is often not discounted, and the content itself is often reused such as a chapter in one book may appear in a survey or "readings" book. Italie (2000a and 2000b), stated that the desire for electronic textbooks is "apparently stronger than the industry's ability to produce them" but Italie also pointed out that issues such as royalty payments to authors, reading on a screen for long periods, and copyright may prevent the growth of electronic textbooks.

Reasons Why Electronic Textbooks Will Succeed

The reasons that electronic textbooks will succeed are:

- As described in *Chapter 2: Once and Future History of eBooks*, when users read reference and textbooks, they are performing deep reading, which is best accomplished by reading from paper. However, for finding information quickly or performing a specific task, then users want to be able to search an electronic book. Thus, for textbooks, students will want to be able to look for information quickly using the electronic version but for deep reading, they will want a paper version. However, if they are only reading portions of an electronic book, then they may not require the paper version.

- Textbooks command a high price and are not often discounted. Even though large retailers, such as Barnes and Noble, are now selling textbooks, both new and used, there is usually very little discount of the retail price. Though discounts up to 20 percent are offered for some textbooks; discounts are not common. Given the current pricing models for electronic books, which is that the hard copy price and eBook price are usually the same, electronic textbooks offer an opportunity to sell books at a high price.

- Students usually have the computer equipment, such as a laptop or Personal Digital Assistant to view the textbook. Many universities require students to own a laptop and this eliminates a barrier as there is less of an argument about having to buy a device just to read an electronic textbook.

- Textbook authors can update their books more often in electronic format. Part of the reason is that typical print runs for a textbook require a considerable period to recoup the print costs and thus it is not economical neither to issue a second edition or make changes to correct information. With electronic textbooks, authors can update more frequently and not be limited by the economics of print runs. (Of course, this benefit also applies to print on demand books, see *Books on Demand* for more information.)

- Textbook content can be integrated with course materials. An instructor, assuming they have the permission of the author, could annotate an electronic textbook with their course material. A more likely scenario is that the instructor's notes would be available in electronic format along with the electronic textbook but not as part of the electronic textbook.

- The growth of distance education, where all of the course content is delivered online in electronic format, is a natural ally of electronic textbooks. In the future, we may see a merger of electronic textbooks with distance education. It makes good sense that not only can the textbook be integrated into the course, it can perhaps become the course.

- Dedicated electronic book hardware readers, like GoReader, designed specifically for the textbook market, have been launched. GoReader advertises itself as the "first company to offer eTextbooks on a portable device specifically designed for the higher education market..." (GoReader, 2000). GoReader claims that its device can hold "an entire degree's worth of textbooks". It eliminates standing in bookstore lines and provides students the ability to create a personal library of their textbooks, course notes, and supplementary material in one convenient place.

The Backpack May Not Go Away

Students stated in a study conducted by Kent State University (Wearden, 1998) that they would be willing to use electronic textbooks and eBooks if they believed that they could read the eBooks on any device as they can use with a CD ROM or DVD.

Besides the issue of standards for eBook content, another drawback mentioned in *Chapter 2: Once and Future History of eBooks* is that users "deep read" a textbook which is best supported by paper and thus if students are required to read an entire textbook, they will prefer paper. On the other hand, if they are only reading a chapter, then the electronic format may suffice. Other factors that may limit the growth of electronic textbooks are as follows:

- Print on demand (also called books on demand) is a direct competitor as colleges are already enabling students to print course packs and textbooks using their local college copy center. Entire books or chapters of books can be stored digitally and printed along with course notes when the student needs the material. The digital content can also be updated frequently.

- Royalty payments are an issue and are complex as, often, textbooks contain content that is owned by many authors so the idea of creating course packs made up of chapters from several textbooks will require the use of a DRM solution.

All in all, students are probably the most receptive users of electronic books and if a business model can be developed where students can buy "collections" of chapters organized into a library for a class, then authors, publishers, and students should all benefit.

Student and Instructor: Book Blues

As a Ph.D. student, I know the pain or the blues of having to buy many textbooks for a course and then only needing to read a chapter or two, or having, to thumb through a 1,200 page book looking for every citation on usability design and wishing I could search an electronic version. For a collection of chapters, I would certainly be willing to pay more than for a single book but would also expect not to pay as if I had bought each book. I hope that a publishing model will emerge that supports this scenario.

As an instructor, I have heard my students complain about having to buy several textbooks because I did not reference each book in each class or each quiz. But the reality is, in one textbook, there might be a few chapters or even tables or illustrations you want students to read, so you recommend the entire book as you cannot copy that chapter and add it to your course materials. As an instructor, I would like very much to choose from many textbooks to build students a "greatest hits" of reference material. As stated above, a publishing model may emerge that supports this scenario.

Xanadu and Beyond

As stated earlier, from existing mediums, new mediums of communicating emerge. Moreover, in some cases, old ideas may make a comeback with new technology.

Ted Nelson, who coined terms like hypertext, hypermedia, and micro payments, proposed, in 1960, an electronic publishing system called Xanadu that actually foreshadowed the need for DRM.

The *Economist* (2000) magazine provided a succinct description of Xanadu: "Xanadu allows the direct inclusion of parts of other documents which are fetched as and when needed. The Xanadu system could contain only one copy of a particular novel. Anyone quoting from that novel in an essay would "transclude" the relevant passage; it would be fetched from the original document whenever somebody else called up the essay."

A key difference between typical construction of information on websites and Xanadu is that websites are collections of documents hung together with links from one document to the next whereas in Xanadu as the *Economist* states: "...consist of original material [such as a book] combined with transcluded bits of other documents [such as a book review]".

What is most fascinating about Nelson's system is that if you could maintain one book and "transclude" content in and out of it, you could easily track usage by users. Users could be charged according to what parts they read or perhaps even the right to "transclude" material from that book to another book.

Nelson provided a guideline on how publishers and service providers could make money in today's nascent electronic book industry. Acording to the *Economist*, Nelson's plan was that "publishers posting documents into the Xanadu system would be able to specify a tiny payment (micro payment) that would be charged to anyone viewing part of the document."

In order for Xanadu to reach the marketplace, Nelson (1999) stated that these "concepts" were needed to enable Xanadu to be implemented. What is interesting about these concepts or issues is that these are all issues that affect the acceptance of electronic books.

• Transcopyright, which is: "enabling legal doctrine, endorsed by lawyers, to enable unfettered virtual transpublishing without negotiation". Simply put, there will be a need for cooperation between all rights holders to ensure that content can be shared between books. Consider the cooperation needed to enable new textbooks to be created from many textbooks for devices like GoReader.

- Transpublishing, which is the "delivery of quotations from [online] publisher (or some virtual equivalent). This requires transquotation servers which will deliver small selections on request". This refers, for example, to the ability to be able to quote a section from one book by pulling in that material from the quoted book into another book.

- "Long-term guaranteed publishing (this is not a technical issue, but a business promise, comparable to insurance)." If one book is used as a sort of central responsibility from which quotations can be pulled from the book will require persistence publishing. Consider how many webpages are no longer available and in the Xanadu system, you will need to have the promise that the book will persist for a long time.

- "Address servers allowing content itself-- not merely closed titles--to have a plurality of address locations..." If you are going to pull quotations from one book, then does each quotation need a separate address so that it can be located on the Internet?

- "Micropayment, which may be interposed before delivery." This is not much of an issue anymore, as technology exists to manage the transactions of eCommerce.

Although, the actual Xanadu system is unlikely to be implemented, the concepts expressed by Ted Nelson and his Xanadu project foreshadowed some elements, and more importantly, issues associated with electronic book publishing.

As McLuhan predicted, the book will become a package of information designed for individual users, and Xanadu's concept is fundamentally a method for users to extract parts of a book or many books to build the book they want.

The gist of this section is that new forms of the book will evolve and these forms may indeed become successful. Some of these new forms, which have already been defined by the OEBF, may include features such as views, tours, and guides.

Book Views

Views can present the content of the book based on a user's interest. For example, a user's view might be everything in this book about Digital Rights Management. A user could select the DRM view and display all of the pages in this book that describe DRM. Another view might be all the comments or book reviews by critics and, most importantly, users.

This concept is already in use with applications like Adobe Acrobat Reader and Microsoft Reader, and electronic book readers like the Rocket eBook, which enable users to view all annotations or comments. But in these instances, these are limited to well-defined data structures or type such as annotations. Until all data is packaged into well-defined structures, which is the promise of XML, then it will remain difficult to present data based on a user's interest.

For example, all text related to DRM would have to be encapsulated with a data entity called DRM, so that those data entities could be grouped together for presentation to the user as the "DRM view". A user would enter a keyword, such as DRM, and then be presented with sections of the book that described DRM. Note that book views and book tours, which are described below, do not provide the same function. Book tours are more useful for navigating through information whereas a book view is more analogous to sorting information based on type.

Book Tours

Tours, which are already part of the OEBF Publication Structure 1.0.1 specification, can provide users with an author's tour of the book or can provide a method to navigate through the book. The OEBF (2001) defines a tour as "much as a tour-guide might assemble points of interest into a set of sightseers' tours, a content provider [or author] may assemble selected parts of a publication into a set of tours to enable convenient navigation".

Using an example provided in the OEBF Publication Structure 1.0.1 (2001) an electronic cookbook might include several tours such as a tour of chicken recipes and another tour of vegan recipes. The tour would link various sections together (as many as the author wanted) to enable the user to view all of the chicken recipes, such as chicken fingers and chicken *a' la king* or view all of the recipes, such as lentil casserole, that are part of a vegan's diet.

Tour or Index?

What is the difference between using a tour or an index to find information? After all, a comprehensive index can enable users to view all of the chicken recipes as well as a tour. For example, in a comprehensive index, you would expect to find an index entry for chicken with every chicken recipe listed underneath it, as well as index entries for chicken fingers and chicken *a' la king*.

A key difference is that tours are prepackaged selections of content that a user can simply select and then drill down to read the information. Using an index requires the user to find an index entry they want and then to select that entry, read the content, and then return to the index if they need more information. Indexes are very effective in finding specific "chunks" of information whereas a tour represents a package of information chunks.

Tours can be effective in promoting a book as an author can define a tour that highlights a character, a city, or whatever topic the author believes will draw the attention and interest of the user. It is very possible that a key selling feature of electronic books will be for users to be able to "tour" the book before they buy.

Book Guides

A book guide is defined in the OEBF Publication Structure 1.0.1, (2001): "...identifies fundamental structural components of the publication...to provide convenient access to them". The structural components are the familiar and useful: table of contents, list of figures, list of tables, index, and other elements as defined by the *Chicago Manual of Style*, 13th edition."

The complete list of elements includes: cover, title page, table of contents, index, glossary, acknowledgements, bibliography, colophon, copyright page, dedication, epigraph, foreword, list of illustrations, list of tables, notes, and preface.

The purpose of a book guide is similar to a book tour; the book guide packages together structures that a user would normally use to find information or navigate through a book. By packaging these elements together, users can drill down to navigate through the book.

New Mediums?

Part of my responsibilities at IBM had been to review suggestions by people who submit product ideas to IBM for electronic books or electronic publishing. Ideas have ranged from new electronic book readers to concepts for electronic book formats to electronic books that read to the user. What has been interesting is that the ideas that have flowed, electronically, across my workstation, have all been extensions of the book and thus, from my viewpoint, validate the premise that the previous medium provides the new medium.

Books on Demand

CAP Ventures (2001) stated that within five years, 80% of all print will be ordered via the World Wide Web and they predicted that a fundamental change will occur with the way books are sold: "...books will increasingly be sold then printed or presented as opposed to being printed and then sold."

Books on demand, which is often referred to as print on demand, has experienced growth for the same reasons that use of electronic books has grown: distribution, technology, and, unlike electronic books, profit. Books on demand can be defined as the use of a digital printer to print a paper book when needed in quantities ranging from one copy to hundreds of copies. Typically, the book is stored in digital format, usually as a collection of PDF, PostScript, or TIFF files, that can be printed on a digital printer and then packaged (such as bound or shrink-wrapped) and then shipped to the customer directly from the printer. Not only can the book be printed one at a time but also the book can be printed in black, white, or color using digital color printers. For example, a single copy of a 300-page book can be printed in less than one minute and bound in less than five minutes (IBM, 2000).

Use of Digital Printers

The use of digital printers, which are defined as printers that accept a digital data stream as input and output printed pages (Hoffmann, 1999), has been growing in the print industry and in turn is fueling books on demand. Digital printers include:

- Direct imaging digital offset, which are offset presses that enable digital content to go directly to the press. These types of printers require less make-ready time than do traditional offset printer and thus offer both quicker time from start to finish for a print job and provide economy for longer print jobs (Hoffmann, 2000).

- Electrographic printers which use a Xerography process to create images. These are laser printers that fuse toner on paper. These are the most common types of digital printers used in the books on demand or print on demand process. These types of printers can support, black and white, as well as full color printing.

- Ink jet printers. These printers are typically used for wide format paper such as posters and are not used for books on demand.

One reason for the increased use of digital printers is the length of print jobs dropped by 25% during the 1990s (Hoffmann, 2000). Shorter print jobs mean less efficiency for traditional offset lithography printers because of setup or make-ready time and paper waste. (Shorter print jobs also mean more time scheduling jobs for printing along with the associated setup time.)

Digital printers, which can efficiently print one job at a time, do not require make-ready time and significantly reduce paper waste. Furthermore, the time from start to finish is quicker on digital printers for reasons such as time does not have to be allocated for ink to dry before post-processing, such as binding, can begin. These are important reasons why printers who traditionally publish books using offset lithography printers are adding digital printers to their print facilities.

Rick Voytko, an IBM expert in books on demand, recalled how a printer with traditional offset printing presses installed a digital printer because their customers had been asking them to print small quantities of books but, with make, ready costs and schedules, the cost and timeliness of printing small quantities was prohibitive. However, the printer installed a digital printer and thus could handle short print jobs economically and quickly, which opened up a new market. The printer stated that digital printing helped them serve a new set of customers that they could not serve before (Voytko, 2001). Some printers, like RR Donnelley, have moved not only into digital printing but also into electronic books as well, thus the new medium has melded with the old medium.

Workflow Equals Savings

Books on demand (and print on demand) are popular with both printers and publishers because, unlike electronic books (currently), there are clear cost savings for the publisher. The workflow to create a book to be printed on an offset press is the same as the workflow to create a book to be printed on a digital printer. Thus, a publisher and printer could print a book for an initial run on an offset press and then print smaller runs on a digital printer without having to recreate the source files for printing.

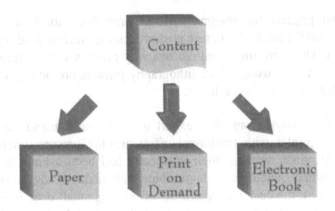

Figure 15: One Source; Multiple Outputs

Minimizing Risk in the Lifecycle of a Book

An important element of books on demand is to understand the typical lifecycle of a book. Voytko (2001) described the typical life-cycle of a book as a bell curve: at the beginning of the bell curve, sales are typically slow as marketing efforts and reviews build demand. Once demand has increased, sales increase and eventually reach a plateau. From the plateau, sales decrease until the book goes out-of-print.

During this lifecycle, the publisher estimates how many books should be printed for the first printing. For the first printing, books are usually printed in quantities large enough to justify offset printing. The books are then printed and stored in a warehouse(s) or shipped to distributors. It is during the first printing that the publisher accepts some risk, actually much risk. If the book sales do not ramp up, and instead of a curve, the book sales are a flat line, the publisher faces returns, which must be warehoused, sold to a discounter, or destroyed. If the sales do ramp up, the publisher may face a decision to do a second printing, and again, the publisher must estimate how many books will be sold, and thus accept some more risk. Eventually, demand will slacken and the book will go out-of-print.

However, when a book goes out-of-print, it may not be because there are no customers or backorders for the book, instead it may be too expensive to print a quantity of books using an offset press. Even if there are customers and backorders for a book, traditionally, the number must be large enough to justify offset printing. This is where books printed on demand on digital printers can extend the lifecycle of a book indefinitely.

IBM (2000) provided this description about the benefits of books on demand: "For books nearly or completely out-of-print, the technology represents a new lease on life. A book in low supply can be downloaded from electronic storage and digitally printed in the desired amount. An extant copy of an out-of-print book can be acquired from a library, warehouse, or private source, and can be scanned, printed, and digitally stored." Thus the bell curve flattens out endlessly and a book need never go out-of-print.

Voytko (2001) summed up books on demand by stating: "The real benefit of books on demand is that publishers can better manage the lifecycle of a book and reduce their risk while enabling authors to gain incremental sales that would have ended when the book went out-of-print."

Benefits for Authors and Publishers

Because the technology provides a cost-effective method to print small quantities of books, authors and publishers can realize the following benefits:

- Publishers can build books to order. Publishers do not have to estimate how many books to print; they can print the books as orders come in. In essence, publishers now have just-in-time-manufacturing, which was not possible with offset printing.

- It eliminates warehouse costs. Most business models for books on demand are based on centralized print facilities where orders come in for books, the books are printed, and then shipped immediately. This eliminates warehouse costs for stocking books.

- It enables niche publishing because the fixed costs of printing the book are considerably less than the fixed costs of offset printing and small quantities of books can be printed at costs far less than offset printing.

- It complements electronic books as the workflow for publishing an electronic book and a paper book are very similar. Once the content is written, the content can be converted into a format, such as PDF, PostScript, or TIFF, files that can be stored electronically for printing.

- It eliminates out-of-print books as a book can be printed when needed. This enables established authors to offer their books again to their audience and enables publication of books that are in the public domain. (An issue with this is that if an author's book never goes out-of-print because the book can be stored digitally and printed when needed, then the rights to that book would not revert back to the author as is the case when the book goes out-of-print. This is an issue for authors, agents, and publishers to sort out.)

Customization of Books

A feature of books on demand that can drive acceptance is the ability to customize the book before printing it. This customization is often referred to as variable publishing. Here are some examples of how books that are stored in digital format for printing on a digital printer can be customized:

- The user wants their name inscribed on the front cover or wants a unique cover customized with whatever images or text they choose.

- The publisher offers the user a choice of covers for the book.

- The publisher offers the user the option to select which parts of the book they want to print. If the book is a reference book, the user might only want to buy specific chapters.

- The publisher offers to combine the college textbook with class lecture notes and materials, which are often referred to as course packs. Many colleges now offer course packs to students via print on demand; these course packs could easily be combined with the textbook into one printed package.

- The user pays the author to add unique content to the book written specifically for the customer. For example, the user is buying a motivational book for their company; they may ask for the book to be printed with a chapter on their company's history.

What is the Difference?

At the NIST conference, *Electronic Book 2000: Changing the Fundamentals of Reading*, I participated in the conference as an exhibitor where I described the IBM books on demand solution. I was surprised by a few things:

Most people were not aware of books on demand. I assumed everyone was familiar with the technology that enables a single book to be printed, economically and quickly, from a digital printer. The majority of people I spoke with assumed all books were still printed in large quantities on large offset printers with ink, and not on digital printers with toner. The idea that it is possible to print a single book with a quality that matches offset printing was quite a surprise

When people looked at examples of books that were printed on a digital printer, they could not tell the difference between digital and offset printing. They were also impressed that not only were the pages printed digitally but so were the covers, in multiple colors.

The new wave of booksellers and distributors who offer electronic books were very interested in books on demand as they have discovered that many customers who shop on the Internet for books want a choice between electronic and paper or both. Interest in electronic books often fuels interest in the paper version too. Like electronic books, books on demand provides an economical solution to fulfilling requests for niche books as well as "out-of-print" books.

World Library of the Future

First, the title of this section pays homage to the World Library Corporation who published the *Electronic Classical Library* and *The Story of Civilization*, perhaps two of the very best eBooks published to date. (During a business trip to beautiful Irvine, California, some years ago, I walked a few blocks from my hotel and stumbled upon the World Library headquarters, and thus was able to pay my respect to these pioneers who alas are no longer in business.)

Libraries, such as the Santa Monica and Los Angeles public libraries have begun to offer online reference library support where users can submit questions and get responses from the librarians. The Library of Congress is also planning to offer online research by e-mail in 2001 (Kinik, 2001). These libraries are considering offering 24 hours a day, 7 days a week live reference support to their patrons.

This leads us to eBooks and the ascendance of librarians. In *Chapter 7: A New Print Economy?* there was a discussion about who will serve as the arbitrators of quality in publishing? Simply put, as authors become self-publishers, as subsidy publishers grow, and as traditional publishers sponsor more first-time authors, who will sort out the wheat from the chaff? Libraries and librarians can help perform this role for two reasons:

1. New business models are emerging that will enable libraries to "stock" more books than ever before because these books will be in electronic format.

2. Librarians have always acted as "filters" of books as they only have so much space and money to buy books, so they must choose which books will best serve their patrons.

New Library Models

Companies like NetLibrary (located in Boulder, Colorado, a few miles from my home in scenic Niwot, Colorado) have created a business model where paper books are converted into eBooks and then sold to libraries who can loan the eBook to a patron, just like they would loan a pBook. This business model, when the prices of eBooks decline, will enable libraries to offer hundreds, if not thousands of books, to their patrons that they could not have offered before. Libraries will not have to provide shelf space, but instead, will only need to add disk space or rent disk space from vendors like NetLibrary to store eBooks.

Librarians as Filters of the New Publishing Model

As content becomes more readily available from many publishing sources, and because of the potential for libraries to offer hundreds, perhaps thousands, of eBooks, librarians can assume a key role in enabling authors to reach an audience that they might not have reached before. Thus, astute authors, regardless of how their eBook was published, may want to market their eBook directly to libraries.

Appendix A: Sorting through the Standards

"Standardization is the solution of last resort, an admission we cannot solve the problems in any other way. So, we must all at least agree to a common solution." Donald Norman, *The Design of Everyday Things*, 1988.

Importance of Standards: A Last Resort?

It is worthwhile to understand what standards are available that define the format of electronic book source files, and what these standards mean to the industry. The industry, led by the AAP and the OEBF, are working to define a common solution.

The importance of standards for electronic books is somewhat disputed in the industry. Hilts (2000) stated that the "[electronic book] industry is nowhere near establishing a common eBook format that will permit consumers to read any eBook on whatever device they happen to own". While the OEBF has been making progress, some critics have stated that standards are not needed, as the industry will dictate standards by the acceptance or popularity of hardware readers and software applications. These critics believe that there are only a few formats, such as Adobe Acrobat PDF, Microsoft Reader LIT, and Gemstar REB, that are viable and the cost of converting content into one of these few formats is not significant. Critics state that authors and publishers may simply choose to support one format and not the others.

Other industry experts believe survival of the fittest will rule and point to the emergence of the VCR video recording system in the 1980s when two formats were marketed: Beta and VHS. Eventually consumers chose the VHS format. The reason was VHS provided more recording time and thus consumers selected the VHS format.

An important note: at the time blank tapes were very expensive, thus longer recording time was very important. As a consumer who had owned both a Beta and VHS VCR, the Beta format was perceived as providing better recording quality but, as time went on, two factors emerged that persuaded me to move from Beta to VHS:

1. The cost of blank tapes dropped more quickly for VHS.

2. Content providers, the people, in movies and television, offered more content on VHS.

The Beta/VHS wars point out a few important considerations for today's nascent electronic book industry:

1. What formats do manufacturers support? What is interesting is that, momentarily, manufacturers all have their own proprietary formats but how long can that last? Will content drive what formats are provided?

2. What do the content providers (the publishers)? Given the active role of the AAP in conjunction with the OEBF, publishers it seem do want a standard and do not want to support multiple formats.

3. Is there a format that provides more value? Some might say that Adobe Acrobat PDF is that format because PDF files can be used for pre-press, press, print on demand, and electronic books. But if viewing online, Microsoft Reader certainly offers an alternative.

Reader Wars

Some people may compare the contest between Adobe''s Acrobat Reader and Microsoft's Reader to be like Beta versus VHS conflict but it is not the same, hence both can win. The reason is that both companies give away their eBook reader, so do users care if they need to keep two, free, eBook readers installed on their workstation? In the Beta and VHS conflict, companies did not give away free VCRs so, once you purchased a VCR, you were locked into buying only media that your VCR supported.

The VCR conflict was really decided by content creators ("the movie people") choosing to distribute content in VHS format and not Beta. In the eBook reader war, the number of content creators is much larger than the "movie" business and the cost of creating content in different formats is not inexpensive but neither a huge burden either (compared to supporting different formats for movies), thus both eBook readers will have access to tremendous amount of content. What will be important is how these eBook readers are supported by hardware readers, like Rocket eBook (now Gemstar) and others. This is why standards, like OEBF are very important, as the ability to display an eBook on a hardware reader is similar to playing a movie on a VCR. Today, we have a standard for videotapes, called VHS; in the future, we will see wide acceptance of the OEBF standard.

Of course, a caveat to this argument is that the content producers (publishers) may not want to produce books in multiple formats just as movie companies did not want to produce both Beta and VHS version. There are two reasons the above argument still holds up:

1. Most publishers produce a PostScript file for print (this assumes printing is around for a few more years, which is a good assumption) and if they have a PostScript file, they can create a PDF file.

2. Publishers may be willing to produce a couple of formats: OEBF and PDF with the reason that one format supports print and the other may be perceived as better suited for electronic display on many output devices.

What can be said with some surety is that publishers will not want to support multiple formats as creating files is not their reason for being in business. If there is not cooperation within the industry on the structure and packaging of electronic books, this latest cycle in the evolution of electronic books may be another proverbial one step forward, two steps backward.

Do Users Care About Standards?

Probably not but what users do care about is the ability to buy an electronic book and have confidence that they can read the book and multiple devices. A study conducted in 1998 by Kent State University surveyed college students who said they would use electronic books instead of their traditional textbooks but only if they could be assured that the content could be read on any device, like a CD ROM or DVD (Wearden, 1998b).

Although users may or may not know about standards, they expect industry to work together to ensure that their investment in technology and more importantly, content, whether a fax machine, modem, or eBook hardware reader, will enable them to move from one device to another. Users will also care about standards if they believe that the lack of standardization will result in costs that are passed onto them. If publishers have to create several different versions of the same book to reach all potential users, then the publishers will pass on those costs to the users and users will not support such a business model.

Are there Rules and Guidelines to Follow?

The simple answer is yes and no. The reason for this is that while standards have been developed and used by some in the industry, there is no agreement on validating whether an eBook is compliant with the standard. Currently, the OEBF Publication Structure 1.0.1 does not use the word compliant, instead, the word, conform is used, which provides much more leeway for content providers to decide the structure and mark-up of the content.

From an ePublishing perspective, it would make sense if there were a brand or logo that could be applied to an electronic book that ensured the content had been formatted or marked up and validated against a specification to ensure complete capability. Some in the industry have argued that with a nascent industry, setting too rigid a standard, such as requiring that the mark-up of an electronic book be validated against a set of rules (referred to as Document Type Definition) would stunt growth. They argue the industry cannot wait as it is more important to publish now and then later, if necessary, convert content into an approved format. Given that there are many more tools to convert content from one electronic format to another, as opposed to converting Beta to VHS tapes, this argument is mostly correct but the longer the industry continues to move forward without a codified, widely endorsed, standard that demands compliance, it may be that users will find their eBooks obsolete sooner than later.

From an author's perspective, all authors need to do is create their source files using an application like Adobe FrameMaker or Microsoft Word and then convert the content into one or more formats depending upon how the electronic book will be distributed. For example, both Adobe and Microsoft provide a plug-in for Microsoft Word that enables authors to create electronic books directly from Microsoft Word to Adobe PDF or Microsoft LIT. Additionally, companies like OverDrive provide sophisticated tools to convert source files, such as Microsoft Word, into LIT format. Furthermore, there are tools from other vendors that authors can use to convert source files into OEBF Publication Structure, 1.0.1. See *Appendix C: Creating eBooks with Microsoft Word* and *Appendix D: Creating eBooks with Adobe Acrobat* for more details.

Therefore, what is most important for authors is to use a tool that:

- Exports source files in HTML as there are tools available which can be used to convert HTML into XML into OEBF Publication Structure, 1.0.1.

- Is compatible with tools from Adobe and Microsoft, which can be used to create electronic books in either PDF or LIT format.

OEBF Publication Structure: A Brief Tour

The OEBF Publication Structure, Version 1.0.1, provides a definition of all the elements that are needed to create a complete electronic book package. It is important to note that the word package is used specifically because not only does an electronic book contain the author's figures, illustrations, tables, and text. It also inlcudes the information needed by publishers and retailers to prepare and sell the electronic book. Consider that when you prepare a book for printing, you are typically sending three sets of files: text, graphics, and a PostScript (or PDF) file. In this case, it helps to send along a note or manifest (or a collating list in the days before PostScript) of the contents to help the publisher and printer prepare to print the book.

The OEBF has proposed a "package" of information that represents the content and information about an electronic book that is needed by publishers, distributors, and retailers. Authors should be aware of this packaging scheme as many vendors have adopted this package and, as there are some parts of the package, such as tours and guides, that the author may be responsible for creating.

Electronic Book Package

The OEBF has defined a book package, which is a collection of items that make up the entire electronic book. These items include: publication identity, metadata, manifest, spine, tours, and guide.

Element	Definition
Metadata	This metadata describes the book. *Chapter 5: Searching for Metadata* for detailed information on the types of metadata that are included in an electronic book and package file. Note: the metadata in the package file and the electronic book are the same.
Manifest	A list of all files that are needed to complete an electronic book. The manifest must include an item attribute for each object and an ID that identifies the type of item, such as text and image.
Spine	A spine provides the reading order of the content in the electronic book and is comprised of references to items, such as

	table of contents, chapters, and so on that make up the electronic book.
Identity	This element identifies the package. For most cases, the metadata element used to identify the book, such as the ISBN, will be used to identify the package and this helps ensure a unique package identity. How to identify electronic books (as well as packages) is an issue that will require attention from the publishing community as there are many schemes currently available but, in any event, each electronic book must include this element.
Tours	A collection of content that helps a user navigate through the book. *Chapter 9: Oligarchy of New Media* for more information.
Guide	A collection of content that helps to navigate or find information in a book *Chapter 9: Oligarchy of New Media* for more information.

Examples of OEBF Book Package Mark-up

The following is from the OEBF Publication Structure, version 1.0.1:

```
<manifest>
     <item id="intro" href="introduction.html"
           media-type="text/x-oeb1-document" />
     <item id="c1" href="chapter-1.html"
           media-type="text/x-oeb1-document" />
     <item id="c2" href="chapter-2.html"
           media-type="text/x-oeb1-document" />
     <item id="toc" href="contents.xml"
           media-type="text/x-oeb1-document" />
     <item id="oview" href="arch.png"
           media-type="image/png" />
</manifest>
```

Keeping Up with the Standards

Here is a suggested list of organizations that are working to provide standards for eBooks and ePublishing. This list is not comprehensive but if you consider the amount of "content" published by these organizations, these organizations are driving the development of standards.

Association of American Publishers (AAP)

A trade organization that has worked with Arthur Anderson (now Accentura) to produce a report on the future of ePublishing as well as work on Digital Rights Management, metadata, and numbering standards. The AAP has joined with the OEBF to develop standards. Website: http://www.bookpublishers.org

Book Industry Communication

An organization sponsored by the Publishers Association, Booksellers Association, Library Association, and the British Library to create and promote ePublishing standards for books and serials with an emphasis on electronic data interchange (EDI). Website: http://www.bic.org.uk

Book Industry Study Group

The trade organization sponsored by publishers, booksellers, and printers in the publishing industry that researches and recommends standards for ePublishing. Website: http://www.bisg.org

Editeur

The Editeur is an organization that developed and published the ONIX international standard that defines book product information for electronic commerce. Much of the current discussion on what metadata belongs in electronic books is derived from the ONIX standard. A key activity from Editeur is the Editeur Product

Information Communication Standards (EPICS) which provides a data dictionary of defined metadata that can be used for ePublishing. Website: http://www.editeur.org

Electronic Book Exchange (EBX)

The Electronic Book Exchange was an organization made up of primarily technology companies who developed a proposed standard for copyright protection and distribution of electronic books. The EBX proposed a methodology to distribute eBook content from publishers to booksellers, distributors to consumers, and between consumers and other consumers and libraries. The EBX working group merged their efforts with the OEBF in December 2000.

Open Electronic Book Forum (OEBF)

The OEBF was initially launched in 1998 with help from NIST to promote and develop standards for electronic books. The OEBF has become the focal point for the development of standards for eBooks and ePublishing. The OEBF includes members from all aspects of publishing including agents, authors, publishers, retailers, and technology companies. The OEBF is working to become a worldwide organization by holding conferences in Europe and expanding membership worldwide. Website: www.openebook.org

---

Keeping an Eye on the Standards

Eventually, the industry will settle on standards and importantly, will require that source files for electronic books are compliant and validated with the standards. The reason is that as the number of eBook hardware readers and application readers increases, it may not be economical for publishers to support a format for each hardware device. Instead, these devices will only read content that is formatted and compliant with the standards. Therefore, authors need to consider this when they select the tools they use to write their eBooks and they need to make sure their publishers can produce content that adheres to standards.

Appendix B: Keeping in Touch with the Industry

"By now, even if you are convinced that eBooks represent the future of publishing, you may well be wondering how you can catch up. The dizzying profusion of ePublishing sites only confuses the issue. Meanwhile, the merry-go-round is gaining speed. How does one get aboard?" Phyllis Rossiter-Modeland, 2000.

Information Merry-Go-Round

There are so many websites on eBooks and ePublishing that it is not practical to catalog all of them for two reasons: 1) many of the websites will be gone, possibly before this book is published (and ePublished); 2) how do you measure quality? For this section, quality is defined as whether the organization is referred to in articles on eBooks and ePublishing.

Public and Publishing Organizations

Here are the key organizations:

Association of American Publishers (AAP)

A trade organization that has worked with Arthur Anderson to produce a report on the future of ePublishing as well as work on Digital Rights Management, metadata, and numbering standards. The AAP has joined with the Open Electronic Book Foundation to develop standards. Website: http://www.bookpublishers.org

Book Industry Communication

An organization sponsored by the Publishers Association, Booksellers Association, Library Association, and the British Library to create and promote ePublishing standards for books and serials with an emphasis on electronic data interchange (EDI). Website: http://www.bic.org.uk

Book Industry Study Group

A trade organization sponsored by publishers, booksellers, printers, and the publishing industry that researches and recommends standards for ePublishing. Website: http://www.bisg.org

Brown University Scholarly Technology Group

This group provides information on the OEBF publication standard and also provides the Open eBook Validator tool that authors can use to validate their content, if the author has written (marked-up) the content in OEBF format. It also provide tools for authors who want to convert their HTML files into the OEBF mark-up. Website: http://www.stg.brown.edu/service/oebvalid/

Copyright Clearance Center

Besides providing services to obtain copyright clearance, the center provides articles on electronic book copyright information. Website: http://www.copyright.com

Editeur

The Editeur is an organization that developed and published the ONIX international standard that defines book product information for electronic commerce. Much of the current discussion on what metadata belongs in electronic books is derived from the ONIX standard. A key activity from Editeur is the Editeur Product Information Communication Standards (EPICS) which provides a data dictionary of defined metadata that can be used for ePublishing. Website: http://www.editeur.org

International eBook Award Foundation

This organization sponsors an award for eBooks that is presented at the Frankfurt Book Trade Fair. The goal of the International eBook Award Foundation is to promote eBook technology and writers who want to develop eBooks. To be eligible, authors must submit a published eBook in Adobe PDF, Gemstar REB, or Microsoft LIT format. Website: http://www.iebar.org

Library of Congress

The Library of Congress is actively involved in converting documents and books to electronic format and has been active in copyright issues for electronic books. Website: http://lcweb.loc.gov

National Institute of Standards and Technology

This is the organization that helped "jump start" the electronic book industry by organizing a conference and then working with key companies to begin development of the OEBF. It sponsored key conferences including *Electronic Book 1999: The Next Chapter* and *Electronic Book 2000: Changing the Fundamentals of Reading*. Website: http://www.nist.gov

United States Copyright Office

The United States Copyright Office has been active in addressing copyright issues for eBooks and is a fountain of infomration on copyright issues. Website: http://lcweb.loc.gov/copyright

Industry Groups

Here is a summary of the key organizations:

Open Electronic Book Forum (OEBF)

The OEBF was initially launched in 1998 with help from the United States National Institute for Standards and Technology (NIST) to promote and develop standards for electronic books. The OEBF has become the focal point for the development of standards for eBooks and ePublishing. The OEBF includes members from all aspects of publishing including agents, authors, publishers, retailers, and technology companies. Additionally, the OEBF is working to become a worldwide organization by holding conferences in Europe and expanding membership worldwide. Website: http://www.openebook.org

Print On Demand Initiative (PODI)

The PODI is a trade organization that was originally created by three companies, Adobe Systems, Apple Computer, and Scitex Corporation, to promote digital printing to print buyers. The PODI group has developed white papers and workshops on digital printing. A few key areas of the PODI efforts are, color digital printing, print on demand file formats, and variable publishing. Website: http://www.podi.org

Academic and Individual Websites

Here is a suggested list of websites sponsored by universities and individuals. Note: the groups selected were chosen based on how long the group has existed and how the organization is referenced within the press.

Chartula

A website devoted to electronic books and distance education. Maintained by the author of this book with emphasis on design and usability testing of electronic books and distance education. The name Chartula is Latin for small pieces of paper. Website: http:www.chartula.com

ebooknet

A website, originally sponsored by NuvoMedia, that provides people interested in eBooks and ePublishing with a place to discuss ideas and to exchange information with guest speakers. It also provides a forum for experts in the industry.Website: http://www.ebooknet.com

ePublishing Connections

A website that offers information on topics specifically on publishing. It provides a list of ePublishing companies and service companies. Its focus is on providing a community of companies in the ePublishing business. Website: http://www.epublishingconnections.com

Inkspot

A website that offers information on topics from books on demand to electronic books. It also provides a place for writers to "network" with other writers and people in the publishing industry. Website: http://www.inkspot.com

Journal of Electronic Publishing

This is published by University of Michigan Press and includes articles on DRM, eBook identification proposals, and copyright issues. Website: http://www.press.umich.edu

174 Electronic Books and ePublishing

Journal of New Media

Sponsored by Kent State University, it addresses many topics such as display technology, print on demand, as well as eBooks and ePublishing.Website: http://ici.kent.edu

PlanetPDF

A source for all things PDF including tools, commentaries, and so on. PlanetPDF works closely with Adobe and often has access to new software, such as Acrobat Reader, as soon as Adobe makes the software available. Website: http://www.planetpdf.com

Appendix C: Creating eBooks with Microsoft Word

There are two simple methods for creating electronic books using Microsoft Word: 1) Microsoft Reader plug-in for Word; and 2) Adobe Acrobat plug-in for Word. Adobe's Acrobat plug-in for Word is described in *Appendix D: Creating eBooks with Adobe Acrobat.*

Microsoft Reader

An important part of Microsoft's electronic book strategy is to make Microsoft Reader pervasive as pervasive as their office applications and operating system. To this end, Microsoft has pursued two paths to enable authors to create Microsoft Reader (LIT) files more easily and inexpensively:

1. A plug-in that enables authors to create Microsoft Reader files directly from Microsoft Word.

2. Cooperation with companies, such as OverDrive, that provide tools to convert Microsoft Word documents into Microsoft Reader.

What separates the free Microsoft Reader plug-in for Microsoft Word from tools provided by companies like OverDrive is the level of sophistication and, most importantly, the packaging of the electronic book for resale. OverDrive, through it ReaderWork tools, not only converts content, including HTML, as well as Word documents, but also creates the necessary package files which contain important information including metadata.

Publishing Tip

If you are planning on publishing your eBook and expect the eBook to be sold through retailers, then you will want to consider using a tool or service that can add information, such as metadata, to the eBook. Version 1.5 of the Microsoft Reader plug-in for Microsoft Word is useful for quickly creating Microsoft Reader files that you can preview and which can be read by Microsoft Reader. However, these eBooks do not contain the important metadata needed for ePublishing and DRM. Therefore, for prototyping or publishing articles or even eBooks that you simply want to distribute in Microsoft Reader (LIT) format, the Microsoft Reader plug-in for Word is well designed, easy to use, and certainly priced right.

Microsoft Reader Plug-in for Word

The free Reader plug-in is easily installed as part of Microsoft Word for Windows 2000 on the Windows 98, Windows NT, and Windows 2000 operating system platform. Once the plug-in is installed, an icon for the Microsoft Reader is added to the Word toolbar. When you are ready to create an electronic book, you select the Microsoft Reader icon from Microsoft Word and your eBook is created in Microsoft's LIT format. The process is straightforward and enables an author to quickly and simply create an eBook.

Using the Microsoft Reader Plug-in for Word

Here is a list of tips and considerations to think about when using Microsoft Reader plug-in for Word:

- Version 1.5 does not handle complex tables such as four columns well. Microsoft recommends that tables be converted into text. You can actually make tables fit but only if the tables are a simple one or two columns in width; tables with more than two columns will not wrap properly. Also, keep in mind that electronic books in Microsoft Reader format are often displayed on Pocket PCs, which means a much smaller display than a laptop so tables will become even more "miniaturized".

- In addition, there are limitations to the number of tables and illustrations that can be included in an eBook which, for example, could be 20 tables and 10 large or 20 small illustrations. (These are the limitations in Version 1.5 and so it is important to read the "readme" file to find out what limitations might apply or might no longer be valid for future releases.)

- Page breaks are nebulous when creating an electronic book. When using Version 1.5, the best results that I have obtained come by removing all page breaks and letting the application determine where the page begins. Microsoft recommends that you set the margins of your document to approximate the "typical" size of the book you are creating. Even though you may "paginate" the book to fit the display by placing page breaks in the book, the page breaks often do not end a page when viewing electronically and you may find it simpler to let the application separate the pages. This approach seems to work fairly well.

- Font size restrictions, which are tables with text smaller than 10 points and the same for diagrams or illustrations with text smaller than 10 points. (Consider that many pBooks are published with text in 9 points; this could be a conversion issue, but 9 points is too small for any medium.)

Suggested Reading

Here are two useful publications available from Microsoft for understanding how to create eBooks using Microsoft's Reader Plug-in for Word. Both of these publications are available online at: http//www.microsoft.com

- *Markup Guide for Microsoft Reader*, October 2000.

- *Source Materials and Conversion Guide for Microsoft Reader*, September 2000.

Appendix D: Creating eBooks with Adobe Acrobat

Adobe's eBook strategy evolved from their leadership in producing tools to create technical documentation and high-end publishing. Adobe created Acrobat Reader to enable business users to turn "office paper" into electronic documents. Adobe added to their suite of publishing products with Adobe FrameMaker, which supports the creation of technical documentation, and the release of InDesign, which supports book and magazine design. Thus with Adobe's experience, developing and selling publishing tools, in as well as their experience in creating the "paperless office", it was natural that Adobe would support the creation of eBooks.

Acrobat Reader(s)

Adobe offers three types of eBook reader applications:

Acrobat Reader	This version provides a limited search function via Find. Otherwise, this version provides the same functions as Acrobat Reader with Search.
Acrobat Reader with Search	Provides the same functions as Acrobat Reader but also provides an advanced search function via the Search command.
Acrobat eBook Reader	This is the former GlassBook viewer and is designed to support online purchasing and DRM technology for eBooks.

Acrobat Features and Advantages

Adobe Acrobat, when used with applications like Adobe FrameMaker and Microsoft Word, enables authors to create fully hypertext-linked eBooks. The advantages of using FrameMaker and Word to create eBooks are that the document structures, like headings, index entries, and author defined structures, are preserved. Here is a list of advantages for using Adobe Acrobat with FrameMaker and the Adobe Acrobat plug-in, called PDFMaker, for Microsoft Word:

- With FrameMaker, Acrobat is incorporated into the product. With Microsoft Word, the PDFMaker plug-in, is added to the Microsoft Word toolbar.

- Headings are converted into bookmarks, which are used as a table of contents.

- Index entries, list of figures, list of tables, and table of contents are converted into hypertext links.

- Uniform Resource Locators (web links) are converted into hypertext links so the user can go from the electronic book to the Internet.

- Cross-references are converted into hyperlinks.

- Page numbers are converted into hyperlinks and which is especially useful with indexes.

- Footnotes and endnotes are also converted into hyperlinks.

- Document properties (information you create, such as author, company, and so on) are converted into document information, which is used by Adobe Acrobat Reader with Search to help locate information in Acrobat PDF files.

A key advantage to using Acrobat with FrameMaker and Word is that the document structures you create can be converted into bookmarks as well as headings. This is an important feature as you may create a document structure or style, such as a heading you might call PartNumbers. With FrameMaker and Word, you can add this structure or style to the PDF file and thus add PartNumbers to BookMarks. This would make it easy for your users to locate information on part numbers. You can also create other structures of styles you need to convey information to your readers.

Furthermore, the ability to maintain document structure, which is a key feature of Adobe's next Acrobat release, enables the eBook to dynamically reflow (resize) so that the page fits the display regardless of the display size.

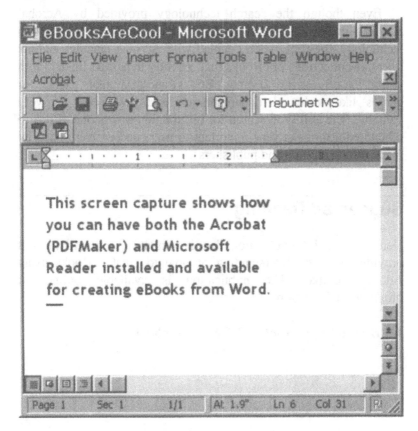

Figure 16: Publishing eBooks with Microsoft Word

Acrobat Catalog

One of the features of Acrobat is Acrobat Catalog, which provides the ability to create a full text search index of the eBook. When combined with Adobe Acrobat Reader with Search, users can perform searches with Boolean operators such as AND which enables users to be very selective in searching for information. The key benefit of Acrobat Catalog is that if you have a set of eBooks that were created with Acrobat, you can index (or catalog) the entire set of eBooks so users can search for a term through the entire collection of eBooks.

Even though the search technology provided by Acrobat Reader with Search and Acrobat Catalog is not the latest in search technology, the tool, when coupled with Acrobat, enables authors to create collections of eBooks that are fully hypertext linked (both within the eBook and to other eBooks) and searchable, which for genres like technical documentation and law books is very valuable. The ability to search for information across one eBook to a hundred eBooks is very important to users and is overlooked by many eBook authors and publishers.

Suggested Reading

Here is a useful publication that is available from Adobe that provides a good understanding of how to create eBooks using Adobe Acrobat. The publication is available online at: http//www.adobe.com

- *How to Create Adobe PDF Files for eBooks*

Glossary

The following are key terms used in this book:

Active Reading

Schillit, Price, and Golovchinsky (1998) described active reading as underlining, highlighting, and commenting on text within a book. Many researchers believe that if electronic books do not support active reading, then the electronic book will never be as useful as a paper book. The tasks of underling, highlight, and commenting can be grouped as annotation functions. See *annotation* and *highlighting*.

Accessibility

OEBF (20001) defined accessibility as "...being usable by a person with a disability where use is facilitated through built-in or Assistive Technology appropriate to a particular individual." Electronic books can provide technology, such as dynamic screen font enlargement and text to audio, to assist users. Additionally, there are technologies on the way which, for example, can convert electronic text to Braille, that offer assistance to users.

Annotation

An explanatory note or comment that can be inserted into an electronic book (Pfaffenberger, 1993). Often, electronic book readers and electronic book applications offer users the ability to create notes or comments as part of the annotation process, these notes or comments, can be exported into separate documents or even searched separately from the text of the book. Highlighting the text is another function of annotation. See *highlight*.

Assistive Technology

Hardware and software tools used by people with disabilities to access content that is not otherwise accessible in their native format (OEBF, 2000). Examples of assistive technology include tools to enlarge screen fonts, Braille readers, and text to audio conversion applications.

Boolean Search

Boolean, also called Logical, operators are used to specify the logical relationship between two quantities (Pfaffenberger, 1993). In search technology, these are operators such as AND, OR, and NOT which enable users to search for multiple terms and include or exclude terms. Many search engines support other operators such as comparison, which includes greater than or less than. Generally most users of electronic books are not familiar with Boolean and comparison operators and thus users prefer to search using a single word, a phrase, or a question. Contrast with *Natural Search*.

Bookmark

The ability to place a marker in an electronic book so the user can select that marker and go to a specific place in the book. Bookmarks can take several forms, for example, in Adobe Acrobat, a Bookmark can be used as a table of contents (bookmarks can be created directly from headings) and also as a way to leave a marker for a page. In Microsoft Reader, a bookmark is used strictly to leave a marker for a page. In either case, a bookmark is usually tied to a specific page in an electronic book.

Books On Demand

See *Print On Demand*.

Cognitive Overload

Cognitive overload is defined by Baecker *et al.* (1995) as the "measure of complexity or difficulty of a task and its demand on [human] resources" and is correlated to a user's learning time, fatigue, stress, and errors.

Completion Time

Completion time is defined as the length of time it takes a user to complete a task from start to finish. If there is an interruption in testing and the user cannot proceed with the task, the completion time will reflect any stoppage.

Copyright

A license that defines who owns the rights to the book.

Digital Rights Management (DRM)

DRM can be defined in two parts: 1) protection via encryption to prevent unauthorized copying; 2) rights management, which can be defined as the enforcement of usage rules. Usage rules include tasks such as whether a user can print the book or loan the book to another user, to more esoteric tasks such as setting a sales price with a begin and end date. Though there is much focus on copy protection through encryption, managing the usage rules is equally important for both the author & publisher and users.

Digital Certificate

The APA (2001) defined a digital certificate as a signed electronic document that binds a public key with a user. See *Digital Signature*.

Digital Signature

Geer (2000) defined a digital signature as a "device that uniquely identifies the sender of an electronic message or document". In eBooks, the digital signature of the author may be used or required to authenticate the content by the author. An example could be that a user obtains an eBook and believes the book has been tampered with or is not the book the author published; one method to verify the book is to verify the author's digital signature. A key point about digital signatures is that a third party is required to manage the data needed to ensure the digital signature is valid. (Of course, the digital signature here is not the same as the physical signature of the author and this raises a question, how do users get their first editions signed of an eBook?)

Digital Watermark

The AAP (2001) defined a digital watermark as "a cryptographic technique for protecting digital content by placing a pattern of bits in the content that is invisible to the consumer but can be read by special programs". Digital watermarks are analogous to watermarks used in paper books. Watermarks have been used before in paper books to classify books, such as draft, or to prevent unauthorized duplication. In this instance, digital watermarks are used primarily to prevent piracy as the watermark could contain, who purchased the license to read the book, and if multiple copies of the eBook were distributed or tampered with, the watermark could be used to determine who purchased the book.

Ease of Use

Shneiderman (1998) defined ease of use as an equivalent term for usability and ease of use is defined in this book as a measurement of how easy or difficult it is to use a feature or product and is a contributing factor to overall user satisfaction.

Electronic Book

Barker (1993) originally defined electronic books as a "...form of book whose pages were composed not of static printer's ink but from dynamic electronic information." Barker (1993) amended that definition to state that electronic books are a "...collection of reactive and dynamic pages of multimedia information." These collections of pages represent the content (books) that are read with a reading device.

Electronic Book Exchange (EBX)

The EBX was a group that was formed to define a standard for DRM with emphasis on distribution and packaging. The difference between the EBX and OEBF groups is that the EBX focused on how electronic books are packaged and distributed in a secure manner while the OEBF focused on the publication structure, which defines the electronic book structure, and on requirements to enable the creation, distribution, and sale of electronic books.

Electronic Book Metaphor

Electronic book metaphors are defined as the elements of electronic books, such as a search tool, that are applied to the design of electronic books but that are not based on traditional paper book metaphors.

Electronic Book Reader

Borchers (1999) defined an electronic book reader as: "...portable hardware and software system that can display large quantities of readable textual information to the user and that lets the user navigate through this information". Lemken (1999) provided a definition of electronic book reader as "...a mobile, physical device [used] to display electronic (digital) documents".

Electronic Book Reader Application

To distinguish between a hardware device, such as a Rocket eBook, that is used to read electronic books, and software applications like Acrobat Reader, IBM BookManager and Microsoft Reader that read electronic books, the term electronic book reader application is defined as a software application that is used to read electronic books.

Electronic Paper

Electronic paper is defined as a media, typically plastic, that is embedded with beads or microcapsules. When electricity is passed through the beads or microcapsules, the beads or microcapsules form letters and pictures.

Encryption

Geer (2000) defined encryption as "the conversion of a message or data file into a form that cannot be understood by unauthorized readers...all encryption techniques require at least one key which describes how a message is encoded and how it will be decoded". See also *key* and *public key*.

Genre

Levy (1994) defined genre as a method to classify documents according to the purpose, role, and function. Genre defines how the document should be used based on user expectations and experiences. For exmple, with a newspaper, users expect headline size to indicate importance. Users would expect that a technical product manual would be organized differently from a novel or newspaper and expect to read a technical product manual differently than a novel or newspaper.

Highlight

The ability to mark or indicate text that the user wants to stand out on the page. An example of highlighting as used in electronic books is how Adobe Acrobat (or for that matter Microsoft Word) enables a user to underscore, strike-through, or color a word or set of words. The use of highlighting in this book should not be confused with how search "hits" are highlighted; in this book, highlight is an annotation function.

Hypermedia

Bieber *et al.* (1997) provided a definition of hypermedia, as follows: "a concept that encourages authors to structure information as an associative network of nodes and interrelating links". Bieber *et al.* also stated that the terms hypertext and hypermedia are often used interchangeably. For the purposes of this research, the term hypermedia can also refer to an electronic book as the terms hypermedia and electronic book are used interchangeably in many articles and studies.

International Standard Book Number (ISBN)

The ISBN is used to identify books (but not magazines, periodicals, or serial publications).

International Standard Serial Number (ISSN)

The ISSN is used to identify magazines, periodicals, and serials ti does not include books.

Key

Geer (2000) defined a key as "a string of data used to decode an encrypted message. The length of the key, usually quoted in bits, defines how secure [strong] the key is".

LIT

The LIT is Microsoft's file type used to denote an electronic book that can be read by Microsoft Reader. LIT is an abbreviation for literature.

Metadata

Metadata can be defined as descriptive data about data, which seems like a circular definition but metadata is really data that is included in the electronic book to describe the electronic book. Metadata in electronic books can include basic information, such as author, date published, ISBN, to data needed for search technology (keywords), usage rights, marketing information (such as royalty fees). Metadata is quite comprehensive and an area where standards are needed to define a minimum set of metadata required in an electronic book.

Metaphor

Preece *et al.* (1994) defined metaphor as a method for describing a concept to a user in a more accessible and familiar way. Baecker *et al.* (1995) stated that the use of metaphor enables designers to design user interfaces with "familiar and commonly understood" features that users can understand based on their experience and knowledge.

Natural Search

A natural search is defined as a question posed by a user to find information in an electronic book. The user is not required to know Boolean or Comparison operators but instead asks a question. Then the search technology ranks the words in the question to determine what text best matches the ranking. An example of natural search technology is *Ask Jeeves*.

Navigation

Fillion and Boyle (1991) defined navigation as the route users take to find information in an electronic book. Typical navigational devices that enable users to choose their route to find information include scrolling, paging up and down, using hypertext links, using back and forward links and other tools to move around an electronic book.

Open Electronic Book Forum (OEBF)

The OEBF was formed initially to develop the OEBF 1.0 specification, which is described below. The OEBF expanded to create and maintain standards needed for all aspects of the electronic book industry, such as Digital Rights Management, publications structure, metadata and to work with other groups, such as the EBX. Additionally, the OEBF is also interested in promoting electronic books to both publishers and users.

Open Electronic Book Forum Publication Specification

A specification created by the OEBF Publication Working Group that defines the format and packaging of an electronic book. Often referred to as OEBF 1.0 or 1.1, the specification is the basis for the Microsoft LIT and Rocket eBook REB formats. The OEBF specification represents an attempt to standardize the format and packaging of electronic books so that if the electronic book is created and is compliant with the standard, the electronic book can be easily ported for viewing on multiple electronic book readers and electronic book reader applications.

Paper Book Metaphor

The paper book metaphor is defined as an element of traditional paper books, such as table of contents, that are transferred from paper to electronic books.

Portable Data Format

Portable Data Format (PDF) is a file type used by Adobe to denote a file (or electronic book) that can be read by either Adobe Acrobat or Adobe Acrobat Reader.

Print On Demand

Print on demand is defined by PODI as "any printing that can be accomplished quickly with minimal make-ready (setup) time and quick turnarounds to the customer" (PODI, 1996).

Public Encryption Key

Geer (2000) defined a public encryption key as a two-key system where by a user has a public key which is stored in a public place, which can be described as a secure phone directory, and another user has a private key. When the first user sends a document, the document is encrypted with the user's public key and can only be decrypted with the other user's private key.

Radio Paper

Electronic paper that can be updated using wireless technology. (Judge, 1999)

Reading Comprehension

Foltz (1996) defined reading comprehension as the measure of the factors that influence the ease of understanding text and predictions of how easy it will be to read text. Foltz identified two key factors that influence a user's ability to comprehend text whether reading a paper or electronic book: user's background knowledge and cognitive abilities.

Rights Holder

The OEBF defined a rights holder as an "entity that owns or has been licensed the digital rights for the intellectual property" (OEBF, 2001). A rights holder can be a publisher, a company, an author, an illustrator, and others, and it is important to identify who holds what rights as there may be metadata and usage rules applied to each rights holder. For example, consider an electronic textbook that is comprised of chapters from several textbooks; who holds which individual rights to the entire book and to the chapters?

Rights Specification Language

The AAP (2001) defined rights specification language as a "statement and grammar that can be used to describe the rights association with an electronic book or a component of an electronic book". It is synonymous with usage rules.

Rocket eBook (REB) Format

REB, which is an acronym for Rocket eBook, is Gemstar's file type used to denote an electronic book that can be read by the Rocket eBook.

Service Provider

The OEBF defined a service provider as an "entity that provides an ancillary service such as assisting in the creation, distribution, or protection of the electronic publication or the collection and distribution of consumer [user] information" (OEBF, 2000). The importance of service providers is that authors and publishers will rely on service providers to convert content into an electronic book format and, more importantly, to apply DRM technology to electronic books. For example, a service provider will most likely offer services to add metadata to the electronic book, which can be a tedious but important task.

Screen Font

A bit-mapped screen font is designed to mimic the appearance of printer fonts when displayed on a computer monitor (Pfaffenberger, 1993). With the introduction of Adobe PostScript and TrueType (by Apple and Microsoft), users could reliably select one font that would both print on paper and view well on a computer monitor. The important aspect of font selection is that some fonts, such as Microsoft's Verdana, have been optimized for viewing online while other fonts work better with programs, for example, Adobe CoolType and Microsoft ClearType which enhance viewing text on liquid crystal displays (or matrix).

Super Distribution

The ability for an owner of an electronic book to transfer that electronic book to another user. The transfer could take the form of a loan, or a try-and-buy copy, or a permanent gift. Without some method to transfer the "ownership" rights (or certificate) of an electronic book from one user to another user, typical book usage, such as loaning a book to a friend or donating a book to a library, will not be possible. Another view of super distribution is simpler; super distribution is simply the act of a user sending copies of an electronic book to other users. Those users cannot read the book until they obtain a license or a right to read the book.

Text Reflow

Text reflow is the ability of a page to be resized to fit the size of the display or the amount of display space allocated to viewing the page. Often text reflow is associated with the ability of a book to be displayed on a handheld device as well as on a laptop or a workstation but text reflow is also important when you increase or decrease the space allocated for the electronic book reader application as the page stays proportional to the amount of space provided. Text reflow only works with content that is marked up in a markup language such as HTML, SGML, or XML. Examples of book formats that use markup language include BookMaster, which is an SGML format, REB, LIT, and OEB which all use a combination of HTML and XML.

Trial Bomb

The ability to provide a free preview (or try and buy) of an electronic book that has a start and end date.

Universal Product Code (UPC)

The UPC is used to identify products and is usually referred to as a bar code. The UPC is often used along with an ISBN to identify books.

Usability

Preece *et al.* (1994) defined usability as a "measure of the ease with which a system can be learned or used, its safety, effectiveness and efficiency, and the attitude of the users towards it".

User Centered Design

Preece *et al.* (1994) defined user-centered design as an "approach which views knowledge about users and their involvement in the design process as a central concern". A key characteristic is that any product, whether a television or an electronic book, must benefit from asking users what features they want in the product and how the product should function. However, authors, unless they are writing a peer-reviewed book, may not include users in their "design" process. The features which should be included in an electronic book, such as, table of contents, represent the research from the user-centered design process. The usability research presented in this book was derived directly from interviewing, surveying, and testing users, and are fundamental elements of the user-centered design process to determine their preferences for features and functions in an electronic book.

User Preference

Preece *et al.* (1994) provided a definition of user preference as user opinions that must be collected at each stage of product design and development to ensure that "unusable, unnecessary, or unattractive features are avoided" and that features users require are included in the product design.

User Satisfaction

Faulkner (1998) and Nielsen (1993) defined user satisfaction as the measurement of user attitudes towards the product they are using which is necessary to guarantee that a user has a positive experience to ensure continued use of the product.

Variable Publishing

Variable publishing is defined by PODI as "digital data and thus the output can change from one impression to the next within a single print run. This could be as basic as the now-common practice of changing the name and address on a letter or as complex as customizing entire catalogs based on known interests of every individual recipient" (PODI, 1996). Other examples include creating unique covers for books with a customer's name on the cover, or printing, or not printing, parts of a book based on customer requirements. Variable publishing is also referred to as customized or personalized printing.

Voucher

The Electronic Book Exchange Specification, version 0.8, (2000), defined a voucher as: "A digital object that describes an eBook's transfer and usage permissions and copyrights. A voucher can be passed from one entity in the system to another entity. For example, a publisher can use a voucher to pass the permission to sell multiple copies of an eBook to a bookseller, or a consumer can use a voucher to pass the permission to use a copy [lend] of an eBook for a specified period of time".

Bibliography

Here is a suggested list of articles and books about electronic books:

AAP (2001), *Numbering Standards for Ebooks*, Version 1.0 and *Metadata Standards for Ebooks*, Version 1.0. Available online: http://www.publishers.org

Adobe (2000), *How to Create Adobe PDF Files for eBooks*, Adobe Corporation. Available online: http://www.adobe.com

Aikat, S. & Aikat, D. (1996). Shared Techniques Between Print and Online Documentation, *ACM SIGDOC Conference Proceedings*, ACM, pp. 125-129.

Argentesi, F. and Rana, A. (1994). An Electronic Library for Publishing and Consulting Information Distributed Across the Internet, *Proceedings of the 18th International Online Information Meeting*, London, England, pp. 487-500.

Association of American Publishers (2001), *Digital Rights Management for Ebooks: Publisher Requirements, Version 1.0, Metadata Standards for Ebooks, Version 1.0,* and *Numbering Standards for Ebooks, Version 1.0.* Available online: http://www.publishers.org

Auramaki, E., Robinson, M., Aaltonen, A., Kovalainen, M., Liinamaa, A., Tuuna-Vaiska, T. (1996). Paperwork at 78kph, *Computer Supported Cooperative Work*, Cambridge, MA, US, pp. 370-379.

Baecker, R.M., Grudin, J, Buxton, W.A.S., and Greenberg, S., (Eds.), (1995). *Human-Computer Interaction: Toward the Year 2000*, p. 575, Morgan Kaufman Publishers, Inc., San Francisco, CA.

Baldasare, J. (1993). Designing Easy to Use Online Documentation Systems, *AT&T Technical Journal*, 72(3), pp. 67-74.

Barker, P. (1992). Design Guidelines for Electronic Books, *Proceedings of NATO Advanced Research Workshop on Multimedia Interface Design in Education,* , Lucca, Italy, pp. 83-96.

Barker, P. (1993). Electronic Books and Their Potential for Interactive Learning, *Proceedings of NATO Advanced Study Institute on Basics of Man Machine Communication for the Design of Education Systems,* Eindhoven, Netherlands, pp. 151-158.

Barker, P., Richards, S., and Benest, I. (1994). Human-Computer Interface Design for Electronic Books, *Proceedings of Eighteenth International Online Information Meeting,* London, United Kingdom, pp. 213-225.

Barnett, M. (1998). Testing a Digital Library of Technical Manuals, *IEEE Transactions on Professional Communications,* 41(2), pp. 116-122.

Benyon, D. and Imaz, M., (1998). Metaphors and Models: Conceptual Foundations of Representations in Interactive System Development, *Human-Computer Interaction,* 14(1-2), pp. 159-189.

Bieber, M., Vitali, F., Ashman, H., Balasubramanian, V., and Onias-Kukkonen, H. (1997), Fourth Generation Hypermedia: Some Missing Links for the World Wide Web, *International Journal of Human-Computer Studies,* 47, pp. 31-65.

Binstock, A. (1999). *New Mantra: Usability,* Information Week, N751, September 6, 1999, p1A.

Borchers, J. O. (1999). *Electronic Books: Definition, Genres, and Interaction Design Patterns,* ACM CHI 1999, Electronic Book Workshop. Available online: http://www.fxpal.com/chi99deb/

Borgman. C.L. (1999). The User's Mental Model of an Information Retrieval System: An Experiment on a Prototype Online Catalog, *International Journal of Human-Computer Studies,* 51(2), 435-452.

Bortafogo, R.A., Rivlin, E., and Shneiderman, B. (1992). Structural Analysis of Hypertexts: Identifying Hierarchies and Useful Metrics, *ACM Transactions on Information Systems*, 20(2), 142-180.

Bryant, J.M. (1995). The Electronic Book: A User's Wishlist, *IEEE Colloquium on Human Computer Interface Design for Multimedia Electronic Books*, P9/1-3.

Bush, V. (1945), As We May Think, *The Atlantic Magazine*, 176(1), July, 101-108.

CAP Ventures (2001), *The Future of Book Printing and Publishing*. abstracted. Full report available from CAP Ventures.

Card, S.K., Robertson, G.G., and York, W. (1996). The WebBook and the Web Forager: An Information Workspace for the World-Wide Web, *Proceedings of the CHI 96 Conference Companion on Human Factors in Computing Systems*, pp. 416-417.

Catenazzi, N. and Sommaruga, L. (1994a). Hyperbook: A Formal Model for Electronic Books, *Journal of Documentation*, 50(4), pp. 316-332.

Catenazzi, N. and Sommaruga, L. (1994b). Hyperbook: An Experience in Designing and Evaluating Electronic Books, *Journal of Document and Text Management*, 2(2), pp. 81-102.

Catenazzi, N., Aedo, I., Diaz, P., and Sommaruga, L. (1996). Experiences in Evaluating Electronic Books: Hyperbook and Caesar, *Proceedings of ED MEDIA 96 World Conference on Educational Multimedia and Hypermedia*, pp. 131-136.

Chen, L. and Rada, R. (1996), Interacting with Hypertext: A Meta Analysis of Experimental Studies, *Human-Computer Interaction*, Volume 11, pp. 125-156.

Chen, L. and Willis, J. (1997). Some Issues Concerning the

Creation and Use of Electronic Books, *Proceedings of SITE 97, Eighth International Conference of the Society for Information Technology and Teacher Education,*Volume 2, pp. 903-906.

Chignell, M.H. and Valdez, J.F. (1992). Methods for Assessing the Usage and Usability of Documentation. Available online: http://arnarch.ie.utoronto.ca/publications/waterloo/

Clister, J. (1999). *Electronic Books,* ACM CHI 1999, Electronic Book Workshop. Available online: http://www.fxpal.com/chi99deb/

Computerworld (1999). Author Unknown, *Software Is to Hard to Use: A Group of Users and Vendors is Seeking, For the First Time, To Standardize Ease-of-Use Ratings*, Computerworld, August 23, 1999, 64(1).

Constantine, L.L. and Lockwood, L.A.D. (1999), *Software for Use, a Practical Guide to the Models and Methods of User-Centered Design*, ACM Press and Addison-Wesley

Coyne, P. (2000), *PDF and eBooks: Linking Form and Content*, Planet PDF. Available online: http//www.planetpdf.com

Crestani, F. and Melucci, M.(1998, August). Case Study of Automatic Authoring: From a Textbook to a Hypertextbook, *Data and Knowledge Engineering*, 27(1), pp. 1-30.

Curtis, R. (1999), *NIST Electronic Book 1999: The Next Chapter*, September, 1999.

Curtis, R. (2000), *NIST Electronic Book 2000: Changing the Fundamentals of Reading*, September, 2000.

Deibert. R.J., (1997), *Parchment, Printing, and Hypermedia, Communication in World Order Transformation*, Columbia University Press

Dias, P. and Sousa, A.P. (1997). Understanding Navigation and Disorientation in Hypermedia Learning Environments, *Journal of Educational Multimedia and Hypermedia*, 6(2), pp. 173-185.

Dillon, A. (1994). *Designing Usable Electronic Text, Ergonomic Aspects of Human Information Usage*, Taylor and Francis, Limited, United Kingdom

Dillon, A. (1996). Myths, Misconceptions, and an Alternative Perspective on Information Usage and the Electronic Medium in *Hypertext and Cognition*, Rouet, F., Levonen, J.J., Dillon, A., and Spiro, R.J., (Eds.), Lawrence Erlbaum Associates, New Jersey

Dillon, A. (1999). *Designing Electronic Books*, ACM CHI 1999, Electronic Book Workshop. Available online: http://www.fxpal.com/chi99deb/

Dix, A., Finlay, J., Abowd, G., and Beale, R. (1998). *Human-Computer Interaction*, 2nd Edition, Prentice-Hall, Europe.

Dretzke, B.J., and Heilman, K.A. (1998). *Statistics with Microsoft Excel*, Prentice-Hall, New Jersey.

Dublin Core Metadata Language. Available online: www.purl.org/dc/

Economist (2000a), *Digital Ink Meets Electronic Paper*, December 2000, pp. 9-15.

Economist (2000b), *The Babbage of the Web*, December 2000, pp. 9-15.

Editeur (2000), *EPICS Data Dictionary*. Available online: http://www.editeru.org

Egan, D.E., Remde, J.R., Gomez, L.M., Landauer, T.K., Eberhart, J., and Lochbaum, C.C., (1989). Formative Design-Evaluation of Superbook, ACM *Transactions on Information Systems*, 7(1), pp. 30-57.

Electronic Book Exchange (2000), *Electronic Book Exchange System, Version 0.8.* (The document is not readily available but you can obtain information about EBX from the Book Industry

Study Group, http://www.bisg.org.)

Esperet, E. (1996). Notes On Hypertext, Cognition, and Language in *Hypertext and Cognition*, Rouet, F., Levonen, J.J., Dillon, A., and Spiro, R.J., (Eds.), Lawrence Erlbaum Associates, New Jersey

Faulkner, C., (1998). *The Essence of Human-Computer Interaction*, Prentice-Hall,

Feldman, T., (1995). FollettWP Electronic Books. Available online: http://www.niss.ac.uk/education/hefc/follett/wp/09.html.

Fillion, F.M., and Boyle, C.D.B., (1991), *Important Issues in Hypertext Documentation Usability*, ACM, pp. 59-66.

Foltz, P.W. (1996). Comprehension, Coherence, and Strategies in Hypertext and Linear Text in *Hypertext and Cognition*, Rouet, F., Levonen, J.J., Dillon, A., and Spiro, R.J., Editors, Lawrence Erlbaum Associates, New Jersey.

Garber, J.R. (2000), *Publish and Perish*, Forbes, October 16, 2000.

Gates, W.H. III   (1995). *The Road Ahead*, Viking Books, New York.

Gedge, R. (1997). Navigating in Hypermedia Interfaces and Individual Differences, Technology and Teacher Education, *Annual Proceedings of SITE 97, Eighth International Society for Information Technology and Teacher Education*, pp. 889-893.

Gervais, D.J., (1998), Electronic Rights Management and Digital Identifier Systems, *Journal of Electronic Publishing*. Available online: http://www.press.umich.edu/jep/04-03/gervais.html

Geer, S. (2000), *The Economist Books Pocket Internet*, Economist Newspapers, Ltd, United Kingdom.

Golovchinsky, G. (1997). Queries? Links? Is There a Difference? *CHI 1997*, Atlanta, GA, US, March, 1997, pp. 22-27.

GoReader (2000), product information available at http://www.goreader.com

Graham, J. (1999). Reader's Helper: A Personalized Document Reading Environment, *Conference on Human Factors in Computing Systems*, CHI 1999, Pittsburgh, PA, pp. 481-488.

Guedon, JC. (1994). *Why Are Electronic Publications Difficult to Classify? The Orthogonality of Print and Digital Media*, Directory of Electronic Journals, Newsletters, and Academic Discussion Lists, Association of Research Libraries. Available online: http://www.people.virginia.edu/~pm94/libsci/guedon.html.

Hammontree, M., Weiler, P., and Nayak, M. (1994). Remote Usability Testing, *ACM Interactions*, (1)3, pp. 21-25.

Harmison, M. (1997). *Creating Electronic Documents That Interact with Diagnostic Software for On-Site Service*, available online: http://www2/rpa.net/~harmison/IEEE2.html

Henke, H.A. (1998). Are Electrons Better Than Papyrus? (Or Can Adobe Acrobat Reader Files Replace Hardcopy?), *ACM SIGDOC Conference, Scaling the Heights*, Quebec City, Quebec, Canada, pp. 29-37.

Hilts, P. (2000), *E-publishing: The Wait for an E-book Format*, Publishers Weekly, November 6, 2000.

Hoffmann, K. (1999 and 2001), *Orientation to the Commercial Printing Industry* course notes, Rochester Institute of Technology, Corporate Education and Training. Also, personal correspondence between the author and Professor Hoffmann, January, 2001.

Hsu, R.C. and Mitchell, W.E. (1997). After 400 Years, Print Is Still Superior, *Communications of the ACM*, 40(10), 27-28.

IBM (2000), *One for the Books: Barnes and Noble Launches Print-On-Demand Operations*, IBM order number, G563-0139-00.

Instone, K., Teasley, B.M., Leventhal, L.M. (1993). Empirically-based Re-Design of a Hypertext Encyclopedia, Interchi 1993, April 24-29, pp. 500-566.

Italie, H. (2000a), *Welcome to the Future: BookExpo America is Going Digital*, Associated Press, June 1, 2000.

Italie, H. (2000b), *e-Books: The Next Campus Fad*, Associated Press as published in the Times of India, August 18, 2000.

Italie, H. (2000c), *Electronic Textbooks Gaining Ground on College Campuses*, Associated Press, as published in Rocky Mountain News, September 18, 2000

Italie, H. (2000d), *Ebooks: A Paper Tiger?*, Associated Press, September 21, 2000.

Johnstone, B. (1999), The Dynabook at 10, *Computing Japan*, October, 1999, (6)10. Available online: http://www.computingjapan.com/magazine/issues/1999/oct99/docs/oct99_dynabook.html

Judge, P. (1999), *E Ink's Message: We're Creating a New Medium*, November 16, 1999.

Kawasaki, G. (1997). The Beauty of Metaphor, *Forbes Magazine*, August 25, 1997, p. 84.

Keep, C. and McLaughlin, T., *Sony Data Discman*, 1995. Available online: web.uvic.ca/~ckeep/hf10014.html.

Kenner, H. (1984), McLuhan Redux, *Harper's*, November, 1984.

Kidner, S (2000), *Will Paper be Forced To Fold*, April 20, 2000, Guardian Unlimited, http://www.guardianunlimited.co.uk/

Kimball, R. (1999). *The Second Revolution of User Interfaces*, Intelligent Enterprise, August 24, 1999, 12(2), p. 54.

Kinik, K. (2001), *The Library That Never Closes*, Forbes ASAP, February 19, 2001.

Kirkpatrick, J. (2000), *NIST Electronic Book 2000: Changing the Fundamentals of Reading*, September, 2000.

Klein, A. (2000), *E Ink Writes Its Future on e-Paper*, January 4, 2000, Wall Street Journal Interactive.

Koons, W.R., O'Dell, A.M., Frishberg, N.J., Laff, M.R., (1992), *The Computer Sciences Electronic Magazine: Translating from Paper to Multimedia, ACM CHI Conference*, pp. 11-18.

Landauer, T.K., (1996). *The Trouble with Computers, Usefulness, Usability, and Productivity*, MIT Paperback Press, MA.

Landoni, M., and Gibb, F. (1997). *The Importance of Visual Rhetoric in the Design and Production of Electronic Books: The Visualbook Experience.* Available online: http://www.dis.strath.ac.uk/people/monica/Crete.html

Lardner, J., (1999), *A High-Tech Page Turner*, U.S. News. http://www.usenews.com/usnews/issue/9990906/rocket.htm

Lemken, B. (1999). *Ebook – the Missing Link Between Paper and Screen*, ACM CHI 1999, Electronic Book Workshop. Available online: http://www.fxpal.com/chi99deb/

Levy, D.M. (1994). *Fixed or fluid? document stability and new media*, Association for Computing Machinery.

Liu, Z. and Stork, D.G. (2000), Is paperless really more?, *Communications of the Association of Computing Machinery*, 43 (11), 94-97

Louderback, J. (2001), *Hail to the Usability Test*, USA Weekend, January 19-21.

Louka, M.N. (1994), *A Review of Hypermedia Methodologies and Techniques*, March, 1994 and converted to online in August, 1994. Available online: http://w1.269.1.telia.com/~u269.../hypermedia/review/Review. html.

Lubel, G., (1996). *Book Concept Verification Test and UCD Test Results*, IBM Corporation.

Mandel, C. (2000), *Content Makers Need New Models for Revenue: Report*, Toronto Globe and Mail, November 30, 2000.

Mandel, T. (1997). *The Elements of User Interface Design*, Wiley Computer Publishing, John Wiley and Sons, New York.

Maney, K. (2000), *Reading the Electronic Ink On the Wall*, May 9, 2000, USA Today.

Mangiaracina, S. and Maioli, C. (1995), Building Hypermedia for Learning: A Framework Based on the Design of User Interface, *Symbiosis of Human and Artifact, Proceedings of the Sixth International Conference on Human Computer Interactions*, Tokyo, Japan, pp. 857-862.

Mann, C.C. (2000), *All the World's a Bootleg*, Forbes ASAP, October 2, 2000.

Marcus, A. (1998), *Metaphor Design for User Interfaces*, CHI 98 Tutorials, April, 1998, pp. 129-130

Marmann, M. and Schlageter, G. (1992), Towards a Better Support for Hypermedia Structuring: The HYDESIGN Model, *ACM ECHT Conference*, Milano, Italy, November 30 – December 14, 1992, pp. 232-234.

McAdams, M., (1995). Information Design and the New Media, *ACM Interactions*, October, 1995, pp. 37-46.

McCusker, D., (1998). *The Design of the Rocket eBook.* Available online as a Rocket eBook article: www.nuvomedia.com.

McLuhan, E. and Zingrone, F., (1995). *Essential McLuhan*, Basic Books, Canada.

Merz, T. (1998), *Web Publishing with Acrobat/PDF*, Springer-Verlag Berlin Heidelberg

Microsoft (2000a), *Markup Guide for Microsoft Reader,* Microsoft Corporation. Available online: http://www.microsoft.com

Microsoft (2000b), *Microsoft Reader, Source Materials and Conversion Guide for Microsoft Reader.* Available online: http://www.microsoft.com

Mitchell, W.J. (1996). *Homer to Home Page: Designing Digital Books.* Available online: http://mitpress.mit.edu/e-books/Text_Unbound/text_unbound.html

Modeland, P.R. (2000), *Leaping on the ePublishing Merry-Go-Round.* Available online: www.ebooknet.com

Moggridge, B. (1999). Expressing Experiences in Design, *Interactions,* 6(4), pp. 17-25.

Monk, A.F., (1998). Experiments Are for Small Questions, Not Large Ones Like "What Usability Method Should I Use?", *Human-Computer Interaction,* 13(3), pp. 296-303.

Moll-Carrillio, Saloman, G., Marsh, M., Suri, J.F., and Spreenberg, P. (1995), Articulating a metaphor through user centered design, *Association for Computing Machinery, Conference Proceedings on Human Factors in Computing Systems,* 566-572.

Muter, P. (1996). Interface Design and Optimization of Reading Continuous Text, in van Oostendorp, H. and de Mul, S. (1996), *Cognitive Aspects of Electronic Text Processing,* Ablex Publishing. Available online: http://www.pysch.utoronto.ca/~muter/pmuter1.htm

Muter, P. and Maurutto, P. (1991). Reading and Skimming from Computer Screens and Books: The Paperless Office Revisited, *Behavior and Information Technology,* Volume 10, 257-266. Available online: http://www.pysch.utoronto.ca/~muter/pmuter2.htm

Narayanan, N.H. and Hegarty, M. (1998). On Designing

Comprehensible   Interactive   Hypermedia   Manuals, *International Journal of Human-Computer Studies*, 48, 267-301.

Nelson, T. (1999), *Project Xanadu*. Available online: http://www.xanadu.com.

Nichols, J., Howes, J., and Jones, R. (1995). Information Seeking Behavior Using Paper and Electronic Versions of a Textbook, *IEEE Colloquium on Human Computer Interface Design for Multimedia Electronic Book*, London, England, Digest No. 1995/038, 5/1-5/3.

Nielsen, J. (1990). The Art of Navigating in Hypertext, *Communications of the ACM*, 33(3), pp. 296-310.

Nielsen, J. (1998a, February 26). *In Defense of Print*, available online: http://www.useit.com/alertbox/980226.html

Nielsen, J. (1998b, July, 26). *Electronic Books: A Bad Idea*, available online: http://www.useit.com/alertbox/980726.html

Nielsen, J., (1993). *Usability Engineering*, AP Professional, MA.

Norman, D.A. (1988), *The Design of Everyday Things*, Doubleday, NY

O'Hara, K. and Sellen, A. (1997). *A Comparison of Reading Paper and On-Line Documents*, CHI 97, March, 1997, 335-342.

Open Electronic Book Forum (2001), *Publication Structure, 1.0.1.* Available online at http://www.openebooks.org

Pfaffenberger, B. (1993), *Que's Computer User's Dictionary*, 4th Edition, Que Corporation

Paolini, P. (1999). Hypermedia, the Web and Usability Issues, *Proceedings of the IEEE International Conference on Multimedia Computing and Systems*, Florence, Italy, June, 1999, Volume 1, pp. 111-115.

Parlangeli, O., Marchigiani, E., Bagnara, S. (1999). Multimedia Systems in Distance Education: Effects on Usability on Learning, *Interacting with Computers*, 12(1), September, 1999, pp. 37-49.

Paterno, F. and Mancini, C. (1999). *Developing Adaptable Hypermedia*, IUI 99, Redondo Beach, CA, pp. 163-170.

Perera, S., Hobbs, D, and Moore, D. (1999). Visual Metaphors to Enhance Hypermedia, 1999 *IEEE International Conference on Information Visualization*, London, United Kingdom, July, 1999, pp. 484-489.

Piruoz, R. (2000), *Designing the eBook*, Adobe Corporation. Available online: http://www.adobe.com

Preece, J., Sharp, H., Benyon, D., Holland, S., and Carey, T. (1994). *Human-Computer Interaction*, First Edition, England: Addison Wesley Longman.

Price, M.P., Schillit, B.N, and Golovchinsky, G. (1998). XLibris: The Active Reading Machine, *CHI 98*, Demonstrations, pp. 22-23.

Prince (2000), *Rave Un2 the Napster Fantastic*, Industry Standard, October 2, 2000.

Print On Demand Initiative. (1996), *Selling Print On Demand to Your Customers*. Available online: www.podi.org

Rawlins, G.J.E. (1993). Publishing Over the Next Decade, *Journal of the American Society for Information Science*, 44(8), pp. 474-479.

Ritter, M. (1998), *Electronic Ink Could Change Books*, December 13, 1998, Popular Science. Available online: http://www.popsci.com/news/12131998.eink.html

Rossiter-Modeland, P. (2000), *Leaping Onto the ePublishing Merry Go-Round*, February 28, 2000, available online:

http://www.ebooknet.com

Rouet, J.F., and Levonen, J.J. (1996). An Introduction to Hypertext and Cognition, in Rouet, JF, Levonen, J.J., Dillon, A., and Spiro, R.J. (Eds.), *Hypertext and Cognition*, Lawrence Erlbaum Associates, p. 10.

Rowland, F., Bell, I., and Falconer, C. (1997). Human and Economic Factors Affecting the Acceptance of Electronic Journals by Readers, *Canadian Journal of Communication*, 22(3/4), pp. 61-75.

Rowland, F., McKnight, C., Meadows, J., and Such, P. (1996). ELVYN: The Delivery of an Electronic Version of a Journal from the Publisher to Libraries, *Journal of American Society for Information Science*, 47(9), 690-700.

Rushlo, M. (2000), *Companies Race to Develop Electronic Paper*, December 12, 2000, Upside Today, The Tech Insider. Available online:

Rust, G. and Bide, M. (2000), *The <Indecs> Metadata Framework, Principles, Model, and Data Dictionary*, June, 2000.

Salant, P. and Dillman, D.A., (1994). *How to Conduct Your Own Survey*, John Wiley & Sons, New York.

Schillit, B.N., Price, M.N, and Golovchinsky, G. (1998). *Digital Library Appliances*, Digital Libraries 98, Pittsburgh, Pennsylvania, USA, pp. 217-226.

Shneiderman, B. (1998). *Designing the User Interface, Strategies for Effective Human-Computer Interaction*, Third Edition, Addison-Wesley. Readng, MA.

Smart, K.L., DeTienne, B. K., and Whiting, M., (1998). Customers' Use of Documentation: The Enduring Legacy of Print, *ACM SIGDOC Conference, Scaling the Heights*, Quebec City, Quebec, Canada, pp. 23-28.

Tidline, T.J. (1999). The Mythology of Information Overload, *Library Trends*, 47(3), Winter, 1999, 485-506.

Vaananen, K. and Schmidt, J. (1994). User Interfaces for Hypermedia: How to Find Good Metaphors?, *Conference Companion*, CHI 94, pp. 263-264.

Votsch, V. (1999). Hand Held E Books: the Reality Behind the Hype, *Seybold Report on Internet Publishing*, January, 1999, pp. 8-14.

Voytko, R. (2001), personal conversations with the author. Voytko is a certified project manager and an expert in publishing workflows and books on demand.

Wan, E., Roberston, P., Brook, J., Bruce, S., and Armitage, K. (1999). Retaining Hyperlinks in Printed Hypermedia, *Computer Networks, The International Journal of Computer and Telecommunications Networking*, 31(11), pp. 509-524.

Wearden, S. (1998a). *Landscape vs. Portrait Formats: Assessing Consumer Preferences*. Available onine:
http://wwwjmc.kent.edu/futureprint/1998summer/wearden.htm

Wearden, S. (1998b). *Electronic Books: A Study of Potential Features and Their Perceived Value*. Available online:
http://wwwjmc.kent.edu/futureprint/1998fall/wearden.htm

Widenmuth, B.M. (1999). *The Relationship Between a Book's Genre and the Activities it Supports*, ACM CHI 1999, Electronic Book Workshop. Available online:
http://www.fxpal.com/chi99deb/

Widenmuth, B.M., Friedman, B.M., and Downs, S.M., (1998). Hypertext Versus Boolean Access to Biomedical Information: a Comparison of Effectiveness, Efficiency, and User Preferences, *ACM Transactions on Computer Human Interaction*, 1998, 5(2), pp. 156-183.

Wolfram, D. and Dimitroff, A. (1998). Hypertext Versus Boolean

Based Searching in a Bibliographic Environment: A Direct Comparison of Searcher Performance, *Information and Processing and Management*, 34/6, 669-679.

Woodward, H., Rowland, F., McKnight, C., Meadows, J., and Pritchett, C. (1997). Electronic Journals: Myths and Realities, *OCLC Systems and Services*, 1997, 13(4), 144-151.

Wright, P. (1991). Cognitive Overheads and Prostheses: Some Issues In Evaluating Hypertexts, *Hypertext 1991 Proceedings*, pp. 1-12.

Xerox (2000), *Electronic Reusable Paper*, available online: http://www.parc.xerox.com/dhl/projects/gyricon/

Zajicek, M. and Windsor, R. (1995). Using Mixed Metaphors to Enhance the Usability of an Electronic Multimedia Document, *IEEE Colloquium on Human Computer Interaction Design for Multimedia Electronic book*, Digest Number 1995/038, pp. 2/1-7.

Index

PRACTITIONER SERIES

Series Editor: Ray Paul
Editorial Board: Frank Bott, Nic Holt,
                  Kay Hughes, Elizabeth Hull,
                  Richard Nance, Russel Winder and Sion Wyn

These books are written by practitioners for practitioners.

They offer thoroughly practical hands-on advice on how to tackle specific problems. So, if you are already a practitioner in the development, exploitation or management of IS/IT systems, or you need to acquire an awareness and knowledge of principles and current practice in an IT/IS topic fast then these are the books for you.

All books in this series will be clear, concise and problem solving and will cover a wide range of areas including:
- systems design techniques
- performance modelling
- cost and estimation control
- software maintenance
- quality assurance
- database design and administration
- HCI
- safety critical systems
- distributed computer systems
- internet and web applications
- communications, networks and security
- multimedia, hypermedia and digital libraries
- object technology
- client-server
- formal methods
- design approaches
- IT management

All books are, of course, available from all good booksellers (who can order them even if they are not in stock), but if you have difficulties you can contact the publishers direct, by telephoning +44 (0) 1483 418822 (in the UK & Europe), +1/212/4 60/15 00 (in the USA), or by emailing orders@svl.co.uk

www.springer.de www.springer-ny.com

The Essential Series

Editor: John Cowell

If you are looking for an accessible and quick introduction to a new language or area then these are the books for you.

Covering a wide range of topics including virtual reality, computer animation, Java, and Visual Basic to name but a few, the books provide a quick and accessible introduction to the subject. **Essential** books let you start developing your own applications with the minimum of fuss - and fast.

The next page of this book is devoted to giving brief information about one of the titles in this series.

All books are, of course, available from all good booksellers (who can order them even if they are not in stock), but if you have difficulties you can contact the publishers direct, by telephoning +44 1483 418822 (in the UK and Europe), +1/212/4 60 15 00 (in the USA), or by emailing orders@svl.co.uk

www.springer.de   www.springer-ny.com
www.essential-series.com

Essential
Linux *fast*

Ian Chivers

Linux has become increasingly popular as an alternative operating system to Microsoft Windows as its ease of installation and use has improved. This, combined with an ever growing range of applications, makes it an attractive alternative to Windows for many people.

Ian Chivers focuses on...
- The essential preliminaries that should be carried out before installing Linux
- Installing a Linux system
- Configuring peripherals
- Using X Windows
- Basic and intermediate Unix commands
- Using the Internet with Linux
- Using Linux for document preparation
- Using Linux for programming

If you are thinking of switching from Windows, this book tells you how to get and install Linux and explains why Linux is becoming the hottest operating system of the Millennium.

240 pages
Softcover
ISBN 1-85233-408-8

Please see page 225 for ordering details